Investing
by the Stars

Investing by the Stars

Using Astrology in the Financial Markets

Henry Weingarten

McGraw-Hill

New York   San Francisco   Washington, D.C.   Auckland   Bogotá
Caracas   Lisbon   London   Madrid   Mexico City   Milan
Montreal   New Delhi   San Juan   Singapore
Sydney   Tokyo   Toronto

Library of Congress catalog card number: 96-76040

McGraw-Hill

*A Division of The **McGraw·Hill** Companies*

Excerpts within Chap. 4:
Gann and the Planets, Copyright © 1996 by Greg Meaders.
Long Cycles and the Master Time Factor, Copyright © 1996 by Richard Mogey.
Forecasting the Crash of 1987, Copyright © 1996 by Charles Harvey, D.F. Astrol. S.
Predicting the 1987 Market Crash, Copyright © 1996 by Arch Crawford.

1 2 3 4 5 6 7 8 9 0   DOC/DOC   9 0 1 0 9 8 7 6

ISBN 0-07-068999-7

The sponsoring editor for this book was David Conti, the editing supervisor was Paul R. Sobel, and the production supervisor was Donald F. Schmidt. It was set in Fairfield by Terry Leaden of McGraw-Hill's Professional Book Group composition unit.

Printed and bound by R. R. Donnelley & Sons Company.

This publication is designed to provide accurate and authoritative information in regard to the subject matter covered. It is sold with the understanding that the publisher is not engaged in rendering legal, accounting, or other professional service. If legal advice or other expert assistance is required, the services of a competent professional person should be sought.
>   —*from a declaration of principles jointly adopted by a committee of the American Bar Association and a committee of publishers.*

McGraw-Hill books are available at special quantity discounts to use as premiums and sales promotions, or for use in corporate training programs. For more information, please write to the Director of Special Sales, McGraw-Hill, 11 West 19th Street, New York, NY 10011. Or contact your local bookstore.

 This book is printed on recycled, acid-free paper containing a minimum of 50% recycled, de-inked fiber.

To my clients and mentors:
Past, Present, and Future

Contents

Introduction   *ix*
Acknowledgments   *xv*

1. Yes, Astrology   1

2. Financial Astrology 101   27

3. Know Thyself   49

4. Market Timing and the Art of Prediction   65

5. Selecting Markets   107

6. Astrological Guidelines for Trading   133

7. News and Geopolitical "Surprises"   155

8. Special Situations   165

9. Creating Your Financial Future: A Five Step Program 179

Appendixes

I. Q & A   187

II. Bad Data, Chart Data, Eclipses, and Retrogrades   199

III. Astrological Financial Profile   207

IV. Resources   213

Glossary   221
Index   225

Introduction

How Investors Use Astrology

Today it is an open secret on Wall Street that astrology is "hot", especially since the 1987 crash had been predicted by a number of astrologers. Similar to the technical analysis of 30 years ago, it has yet to achieve maninstream acceptance. Yet some of the most successful traders use it. Many wealthy financiers employ astrological advisors. They know from experience that consulting financial astrologers can help make them money.

People become attracted to financial astrology in a number of ways. Some have a family astrologer who also helps them plan their financial futures. Others hear about a sensational forecast made by a financial astrologer and want to hear more. Many market professionals know about market cycles and want another charting tool. Having been a professional astrologer for 20 years first, it was natural for me to believe I could make money investing by the stars. After all, I had first heard about the 1987 market crash in October of 1986! Furthermore, my background in math and computers facilitated my development of the appropriate trading models to make money from astrological forecasts. More about that later.

Until recently, financial astrologers were consulted only at the time of major visible astronomical events, such as eclipses, or to provide some reporter with an oddball view of a particularly confusing or highly volatile market. Today they influence tens of billions of investment dollars, and major fund managers worldwide regularly consult them for both first and second opinions on global stock, bond, and commodity markets. While astrologers sometimes make mistakes or can be surprised by market behavior, market forecasts made by competent, experienced financial astrologers often are more accurate and precise than other economic modeling systems.

Market professionals, investors, analysts and traders, as well as financial astrologers, find that knowledge of astrology—i.e., Psychology and timing—is as important as technical and fundamental analysis in forecasting market behavior. Please ponder the following five points:

1. Astrology is more than one-half the market. Of the five major potentially knowable factors that influence markets, Fundamental Analysis, Technical Analysis, Market Timing, Market Psychology, and Geopolitical Events, astrological input is needed to calculate and successfully forecast the latter three's influences.

2. Astrology is a mathematical psychology based on astronomy. Astrology is a mathematical discipline, offering investors the option of charting not only cycles and market psychology, but also unique cosmic/terrestrial events. Astrology not only measures cycles and unique events, but projects these cycles and unique events in advance.

3. Astrology can be a telescope and/or microscope. Financial astrologers chart both intermediate and long-range trends, as well as forecast short-term and intraday market moves.

4. Markets have horoscopes. Countries, stocks, investors, and financial advisors.

5. First rule: Look to your own chart (horoscope). One common denominator of successful traders and investors is that each expresses his or her own unique style. Astrology helps one to discover one's personal trading/investing style, market affinities, and timing cycles.

What Does a Financial Astrologer Do?

"Is this a good time to buy IBM?"

"Should I sell my gold stocks, or buy more?"

"It is better to invest in Italy or Vietnam at this time?"

"When will the market crash? Will this be another buying opportunity?"

The two biggest questions investors ask financial astrologers involve stock picking—i.e., *where?*—and market timing—i.e., *when?* Where shall I invest my money? In what industries, in what stocks, even in what countries? When should I buy, and when should I sell? Financial astrologers look not only to fundamental and technical analysis but to horoscopes to find answers to these questions.

Financial astrology can provide you with not only a unique perspective on markets, but also an important edge in choosing the right time to act. My first two forecasting successes are illustrative.

First, I had to establish my reputation as a financial astrologer. But how? The 1987 crash had already been predicted. The obvious answer was Tokyo. *Everyone* knew that market would crash, but they still kept losing their shirt shorting. More than two years in advance we at the Astrologers Fund correctly forecast the week it would tumble. At the same time, we also correctly predicted the Gulf War the day after President Bush was inaugurated for mid-January 1991; the beginning and end of the last recession; and quite a few other forecasts that got us our first story mention in *Barrons*.

Second, I set up the Astrologers Fund, a money management firm, on May 2, 1988. I had my attorney draw up the papers and I personally went to Albany to file them that day. He thought I was crazy, but I gave him lots of business with my computer company and paid the bills on time. The reason:

The next day I *knew* astrology would be in the news—and it was! The Nancy Reagan story broke. For three days my secretary acted as my press secretary. Not only were there many reporters from the print media who wanted to get my opinion of astrology in the White House, there was also a veritable parade of TV interviews from both the local and national network camera crews of CBS, NBC, and ABC.

Certainly an auspicious beginning for an outstanding call record in terms of precision and accuracy, but not 100 percent. We made, and still make, bad forecasts. You may find incredible our batting average in terms of both extremely precise *and* accurate forecasts, especially if you're used to conventional economic forecasting models as opposed to financial astrologers.

First-encounter stories are often sensational. They have to be, to get a rational, experienced investor to *first* look up to the heavens before calling her or his broker.

In my own case, the conversion process was easy, I had been an astrologer for 20 years. Having first heard about the October 1987 stock market crash a year in advance to the day in October 1986 from the English astrologer Charles Harvey, I was able to make the obvious connection between the planets, money, and the markets.

My first million-dollar client came my way due to fortuitous scheduling of our first interview. At the right moment I pointed to my trading screen: the British Pound Future contract had *just* reached a multi-year high of $2.0040. I boldly commented: "That's the top, period, no more. If you were my client, I would be selling heavily *now*." It went up two more ticks to $2.0050, then fell and fell. Today, several years later, that still represents the long term top.

I hope you're wondering *how* I did that! For that is the subject of *Investing by the Stars*.

What This Book Is About

I believe you will find *Investing by the Stars* to be an eye-opening exploration of the financial markets. You may discover new market mechanisms and helpful guidelines for creating and preserving wealth. Readers technically inclined will acquire a few new astrology tools to throw into their technical grab bag. My book is not an autobiography, I won't bore you with lots of details on how I succeeded, failed, succeeded, failed, and then ultimately succeeded in developing my trading system. I will be sharing with you much of the wisdom I have distilled from my experiences learning about the financial markets. I will also try to answer many of the most commonly asked questions about financial astrology.

One such question is "Is financial success *really* written in the stars?" There are a number of Wall Street theories, such as "the random-walk hypothesis," which hold that day-to-day changes in stock prices are by and large unpredictable. Others believe it is impossible to reliably time markets, and therefore recommend income-averaging. Index fund managers maintain that it is difficult to pick stocks reliably, and are fond of citing numerous statistics which show that only 19 to 21 percent of market professionals outperform the market as a whole. I find it an intellectual—and a fiscal— challenge to prove them wrong.

Of course, Astrology does not replace fundamental or technical analysis. But as with the use of technology, once one has integrated it into one's trading and investing decision making, *not* to use it, becomes unthinkable.

Some classic market studies made a case also to hemlines, rainfall in Stockholm, and sunspot activity. Yet few bet on those indicators. Can *you* take financial astrology to the bank? Will reading this book help make *you* rich? As a market professional, I am not allowed to give guarantees. I can only tell you that I have found the risk/reward ratio to be highly favorable.

When I follow the stars, why not come along?

Acknowledgments

My career as a financial astrologer owes much to many.

First I wish to acknowledge the many fine astrologers who passed along a sacred tradition to me, among them Dane Rudhyar, Marc Edmund Jones, Dr. B. V. Raman, and Charles Jayne. I am also indebted to the dozens of teachers and guest lecturers at the New York School of Astrology, at each of whose lectures and seminars I learned many valuable astrological techniques.

To Charles Harvey and Andy Krieger, whose actions in 1987 triggered my transmigration to financial astrology.

To John Trepanier, my first market mentor, who showed me how to listen to what the market is saying and to be aware of the need for a coherent picture in successful forecasting.

To Joel Kurztman, for inviting me to write for the Business op-ed page of *The New York Times*, which proved pivotal in launching my career as a financial astrologer.

To these past trading partners and colleagues; Peter Corey, who taught me how large portfolio managers approach markets and money management; Ming, who drove home the value and importance of choosing the right instrument—especially when competing in trading contests; and Jules Martin, not only for his fine technical analyses but for the great fun we had together challenging the futures markets.

To my early clients, for demonstrating faith in me before I had piled up a long-term track record.

To the many astrologers and friends of astrology who visit The New York Astrology Center, for their good wishes and words of encouragement.

And especially to my lovely wife Susan, for many things: For valuable advice, both taken and not taken, that has withstood the test of time; for the patience to read and reread this manuscript; and for her horoscope combining with mine. 6:12:12 p.m. October 1, 1994, NYC.

Henry Weingarten

Is There Really a Correlation Between the Planets and the Stock Market?

Yes, Astrology

I wish I could claim that every forecast I and every other financial astrologer have ever made was extremely precise, dramatic, and accurate. Many of them, such as my forecast of the Japanese stock market crash or the Gulf War, were; others, unfortunately, were not. Yet I do believe that upon investigation, you will come to agree with me that financial astrology, while not a perfect investment tool, can be an extremely valuable one indeed.

Advance Information and the Road to Riches

Timely information has always provided traders and investors with an edge. But in today's computerized global marketplace, pricing discrepancies are almost instantly arbitraged. That is to say, the price-discovery mechanism of today's market is highly efficient. So much information is widely distributed and already built into pricing that some technical traders claim there is no need to concern oneself with fundamentals at all. Be that as it may, insider information can still be highly profitable; alas, it is in many cases and countries illegal.

This places the greatest premium on "advance" information as a trading edge, and this is why many on Wall Street and in the City of London are turning to perhaps the world's oldest profession: astrology, or divining the future from sky omens. It is a well-known secret that hundreds of millions of dollars (and pounds, and yen) are traded because of full moons, eclipses, solstices, equinoxes, and before other "interesting" astronomical events. Several of the best financial astrologers are unknown to the public as such, but make a living as successful investment bankers and hedge-fund managers. A far larger number have contracted out for star studies. Does doing so make these investors more successful? You certainly won't be surprised to learn that I believe this to be the case.

Still, I do *not* believe that financial astrology will bring you instant riches. It is no such magic bullet. Buying a computer program that incorporates financial astrology, or subscribing to a financial astrology newsletter, or even employing the personal services of a financial astrologer, will not once and for all end your search for the financial Holy Grail. Financial astrology cannot even equal the promise of a promotional mailing that arrived on my desk today. It informs me that I am one of "a select group of traders...eligible to learn...fortune-building techniques [so as to be able] to live the life I dream" and "snare profits of 107%...468%...even 1382% and more on a regular basis." And if I order this comprehensive course *today,* I will find out how easy it all is....

Using financial astrology may not bring you guaranteed trading profits of "107%...468%...even 1382% and more on a regular basis." All one can reasonably expect is a far greater knowledge of the future, and the rewards appropriate to having such foreknowledge within one's grasp.

Who Uses Astrology, and Why

For thousands of years, kings employed astrologers for affairs of state. Today people from all walks of life consult astrologers to receive vocational guidance or advice on affairs of the heart.

Astrology and Love

Astrology can help to shed light on various relationships: boss/employee, parent/child, student/teacher; lovers, marriage partners, business partners; professional relationships with a doctor, lawyer, astrologer, etc. At the moment when we meet someone for the first time, an instantaneous reaction takes place. Technically speaking, at that instant, the "first meeting" horoscope is born. In life it is uncertain how this will develop, or even *if* a relationship will develop. Astrological charting simply provides one with the probable developmental pattern of the relationship in question, as well as its potential.

Of course this is not based on sun sign astrology. It is a far more complicated issue than whether Aries is compatible with Sagittarius, for example. Numerous technical factors must be taken into account in a chart comparison, studying each chart separately not only to learn each person's needs and desires in a given relationship but also to learn how the two interact with each other, as well as how they relate to relationship itself. Timing, of course, also is very important, as we all well know. Our life histories would be quite different had we met our "significant others" at other times in our lives. The place where a relationship transpires also is considered important, and this "locality factor" can account for possible changing fortunes when couples move.

Later we will see that it is possible to astrologically chart your relationships not only for their love potential but their fiscal potential as well. Believe it or not, you have "relationships" not just with human beings but also with fiscal entities such as companies and stocks.

Astrology and Work

It is common knowledge that most people are unhappy with their work lives. Why is this? Whose "original dream" or destiny are they following: their parents', society's, or their *own* horoscope? Clearly, as an astrologer, I believe that it is only by following the *dharma* of one's own horoscope that one can find fulfillment in this lifetime.

The Dictionary of Occupational Titles rates vocations according to five criteria: training time, aptitude, interests, temperament, and physical demands. Astrologers add two important criteria. The first and foremost of these is *astrological rulership*. Dr. Michel Gauquelin has done many pioneering studies in this field, finding for example the dominance of the planet Mars in the lives of sports champions and military men. Other careers naturally had different planetary correlations. Second, the question "What is the best job for me?" is also to a very large extent a question of values as much as a question of astrology. However, in its essence, vocational choice is simply an expression of self. The application of astrology to the choosing process results in greater self-knowledge, and greater self-knowledge leads to a better choice.

Selecting your ideal vocation, especially one that will still serve you well in the twenty-first century, may mean more than just "finding" the ideal job. It may mean *creating* the ideal job, as well as an integrated and realistic plan to implement your career ideal. A horoscope is also of value in providing you with help in making the optimum selection of working environment (e.g., large corporation, institutional setting, small business, independent contractor, self-employment).

As with any other form of astrological counseling, one tries to determine whether the presenting problem is a central or a symptomatic one, and *why* a client is unable to solve his/her own problem. Astrologers focus on the ultimate goal of client growth even as they try to find an optimum solution to the immediate problem, be it romantic, vocational, or financial.

Of course the two perennial themes of Love and Money occupy center stage, but the possible uses of astrology are limited only by your imagination: relocation, weather prediction, and medical prognosis are but a few. If you are seeking a general introduction to astrology, please consult Appendix IV for some book recommendations. If you would like to know why investors and traders in particular use astrology, please read on.

Horoscope Columns Are Not Real Astrology

Before we look at astrology, per se, let us first eliminate from our consideration *pseudo*-astrology, that is to say, so-called sun sign astrology. The most frequent "straw man" criticism of astrology is directed at sun sign forecasting. How, critics charge, can 30 million American Leos all have the same type of day? It's illogical, they claim, and I agree. Daily horoscopes may constitute fun reading for some, but they are *not* real astrology. Apparently they were invented by the English journalist John Naylor back in the 1920s as a way of selling newspapers, and they are still helping to do that today. In many tabloid newspapers, they are the single most-read column.

This doesn't mean that sun signs have *no* value. Consider the following analogy. It is often said that Germans tend to be precise, and the French good lovers. A fair generality, as far as it goes. But no one would claim that *every* German is precise, and *every* Frenchman a good lover. Hardly. It would be even more unrealistic to predict that today every German will have a good day, while all the French should be careful about health matters. Truly absurd, even though there is some truth to generalities about national characteristics. Further, some Germans are *not* precise, while others, let's say German Virgos, tend to be extremely precise. Likewise some people, myself included, fit their sun sign characteristics very well, while others simply do not.

Astronomically, your sun sign refers to the month you were born in. Each calendar year is divided into 12 sections or signs. In Western astrology this cycle begins at the spring equinox with the sign Aries. However, your sun sign is only one out of dozens of factors used to construct horoscopes. Astrologers also consider the placements of the Moon, and the planets Mercury, Venus, etc. Thus you also have a Moon sign, a Mercury sign, a Venus sign, and lots more. Sun signs are so ubiquitous simply because unless one knows some astrology, or has seen an astrologer, one won't know how to answer the question: "What is your Ascendant and Moon sign?" Both are of equal importance to the sun sign.

Consider the following two cases. One person has his Sun in Aries, Moon in Aries, Mercury and Venus in Aries. The second has his Sun in Aries but the Moon, Mercury, and Venus in Taurus. Even non-astrologers will quickly conclude that the first person will exhibit many Aries characteristics while the second will exhibit far fewer (all other factors being equal).

Finally, let us take the example of the New York Stock Exchange. Established on May 17, 1792, it is a Taurus. Likewise, the Tokyo Stock Exchange, set up on May 16, 1948, and IBM, incorporated on May 1, 1958. But does that mean they all move in identical up-and-down patterns? Of course not.

Still, it could be a fun game to check your sun sign stocks. Do you feel anything special about the following stock(s) (the 30 Dow Jones Industrial Averages, by incorporation date) that share your sun sign?

Aries: Caterpillar (CAT); General Electric (GE); Texaco (TX)

Taurus: IBM; Procter and Gamble (PG)

Gemini: American Express (AXP); Sears (S)

Cancer: Boeing (BA); International Paper (IP); Merck (MRK); Minnesota Mining and Manufacturing (MMM); United Technologies (UTX)

Leo: Alcoa (AA); Exxon (XON)

Virgo: Coke (KO); Dupont (DD); Goodyear Tire (GT)

Libra: General Motors (GM); Disney (DIS)

Scorpio: Eastman Kodak (EK); Union Carbide (UK)

Sagittarius: Allied Signal (ALD); J. P. Morgan (JPM); Woolworth (Z)

Capricorn: Westinghouse (WX)

Aquarius: Chevron (CHV)

Pisces: AT&T (T); Bethlehem Steel (BS); MacDonald (MCD); Philip Morris (MO)

Maybe you notice some connection, maybe you don't. In either case, a quick check of your daily newspaper column against the sun sign of your stock will show you in short order that such columns are not reliable investing tools. *Conclusion:* There is a heck of a lot more to astrology than sun signs.

While we're at it, the following are the sun signs of the 30 Dow Jones Industrial Averages by first listing date:

Aries: Eastman Kodak (EK); Exxon (XON); J. P. Morgan (JPM)

Taurus: American Express (AXP); Merck (MRK); Westinghouse (WX)

Gemini: Alcoa (AA); Dupont (DD); General Electric (GE); Woolworth (Z)

Cancer: Chevron (CHV); MacDonald (MCD); International Paper (IP)

Leo: Goodyear Tire (GT)

Virgo: Boeing (BA); Procter and Gamble (PG); United Technologies (UTX); Allied Signal (ALD)

Libra: Coke (KO)

Scorpio: Disney (DIS); Texaco (TX)

Sagittarius: Caterpillar (CAT); General Motors (GM)

Capricorn: Minnesota Mining and Manufacturing (MMM)

Aquarius: AT&T (T); IBM

Pisces: Bethlehem Steel (BS); Philip Morris (MO); Sears (S); Union Carbide (UK)

Note that we have taken the latest listing of ATT, as per a principle enumerated later of always using the last timed incident as most reflective and inclusive of previous times. Interestingly, in this list only Philip Morris (MO) is a double Pisces. Still, the fact remains that I, for one, sure wouldn't play the stock market by following a daily horoscope column. Not if I hoped to win over the long term.

The Astrological Worldview

And now, for something completely different: A quick look at the astrological worldview, including a philosophical detour. Clearly, this is a subject worthy of a major tome, but there's no space for that here. Let's start with a few philosophical points.

Astrology proves without question that we are connected to the universe. The realization that we are not isolated entities will itself automatically lead to fundamental life changes.

There are no bad energies, only energies badly used.

Each horoscope is unique; each moment in time is unique.

Astrology + Common Sense = Cosmic Sense

If you don't change today, your future will be the same as your past.

Learn to walk with your head in the sky but your feet planted firmly on the ground.

Using the horoscope as their primary tool, astrologers focus on the important issues in a client's life. Clients discover why they are confronting a particular situation, and what lessons can be learned from it. If their current forms of life-expression are not aligned to their higher purpose, alternate possibilities are explored. Ultimately, astrology helps a person to answer life's most fundamental question: *Why was I born?*

Three Philosophical Quickies

1. If some "accidents" may be forecasted from the horoscope, how "accidental" were they?

2. If astrology works—and it certainly does in financial markets—what are the implications of that fact?

3. If someone whom you have never met before is able to tell you about your life and aspirations simply by knowing your birthtime, birthplace, and birthday, what does that say about the world we live in? That it is totally random and chaotic? Perhaps in part, but a more logical conclusion is that there is *definitely* some order and predictability in the material world.

Astrologers claim that three basic factors influence your life:

1. Prebirth factors, such as heredity (and possibly reincarnation)

2. Afterbirth factors, such as environment

3. The birth moment itself

The horoscope (Greek: *horo,* hour; *skopos,* map) literally refers to the moment of birth. It is primarily from the birth chart—whether for a human being, animal, or country, or a stock or a derivative—that astrologers forecast the future. Ignore it, and you may be missing a critical factor.

The Five Questions Astrology Can Answer

Frequently, people seek out astrologers when they are undergoing a personal crisis. They want to know "When will it get better?" and "What are my choices?" Usually they are looking for a larger context in which to interpret their life circumstances. Many recognize that astrology can also help them get in touch with their own higher purposes and to open the door to a healthier emotional and spiritual life.

Of course we may not actualize all of our birth potential—most of us don't. In fact you may not even know what your true potential *is*—an excellent reason to consult an astrologer, I'd say. Of course if we're talking about *financial* astrology in particular, you must ask yourself, "Can I afford *not* to see an astrologer?" Keep on asking yourself that, and eventually you'll come up with the right answer. As you read on, you will find many helpful hints to aid you in this quest.:)*

Essentially, financial astrology is used to answer five questions: *when, who, where, what,* and *how.*

When

The most common use of astrology by businessmen is with regard to timing. One often hears that "timing is everything,"

---

*:) Is a Smiley in Internet code. It is used to indicate a joking statement on the Internet.

and to Indian philosophy astrology is Hora Shastra, the science of time. We are all familiar with the passage in *Ecclesiastes:* "There is a time for all things, a time to sow and a time to reap, a time to be born and a time to die...."

But what is it, exactly, that astrologers time? First, the incorporation of a business. This *does* make a difference, as every financial astrologer will tell you. For the moment, please take my word for it. While it doesn't *guarantee* success, it vastly improves the odds. As New Age entrepreneurs reared in the 1960s obtain positions of corporate power, their clear choice is to work in cosmic harmony. Retail store owners hire astrologers to choose their opening day. Marketing companies hire astrologers to choose the launch-date of their campaigns. Hollywood production studios hire astrologers to select the date and time to commence filming. Salespeople use astrologers to time important sales appointments. CEOs employ astrologers to choose the right times to make public announcements and business travel plans. Some company astrologers help their firm decide when to list itself on the stock exchange, while probably even more wish they had done so. Just take a moment and think about it, and you will easily come up with dozens of cases where better timing would be of great use to you as you conduct your business affairs.

Who

The second most common use of astrology in business is in the area of personnel hiring. In 1970 I first met a very successful personnel manager of a large oil company who used astrology very much for this purpose. (His other use of it was to time pivotal stock market shifts.) As a form of second opinion, many find astrology better than handwriting analysis, which is used more in Europe than America. Vocational diagnostic tests are adequate for predicting many job skills, but they don't even come close to matching astrology in terms of indicating how a prospective employee will fit into a group or organization, much less in predicting their probable contribution three to five years hence. After all, you don't think

Baring's Bank hired Nicholas Leeson on the advice of their astrologer, do you? Or Kidder, Peabody Joseph Jett? Or Daiwa Bank of Osaka Toshihide Iguchi?* Of course not, and we are not joking, but quite serious here.

Where

Every real estate agent repeats the same mantra: "Location, location, location!" But just as it is possible for individuals to relocate and effect significant life changes, so too can companies. Astrology can be used to help choose the location of branch offices, where as well as when to set up regional headquarters and factories and choose suppliers, and so on. Of course, economic incentives also are important. But just think how much happier Disney shareholders would have been if they had not selected Paris where and when they did as the site for their EuroDisney theme park. That one piece of astrological advice alone would have been worth a billion French francs alone to initial investors. Or think how differently things might have turned out if astrology had been used to check out Baring's Bank and Singapore; Union Carbide and Bhopal, India; Exxon and Valdez, Alaska. Get the picture? Some of these disasters could surely have been avoided, others at least mitigated, through the use of financial astrology.

What

Financial astrology helps to sharpen the corporate focus, to restructure and set goals by studying a corporate chart, or when helpful, to suggest a business reincorporation or name change. The question of *whether* to proceed with a pondered

---

*In case you don't remember the details, Barings P.L.C. of London collapsed after a loss of more than $1.3 billion because of what it said was unauthorized trading by Nicholas W. Leeson, a futures trader in Singapore. Kidder, Peabody & Company said false trades representing $330 million in fictitious profits were entered into its computers by Joseph Jett, the head of its government bond–trading unit, over a two-year period. Also, unauthorized bond trading by Toshihide Iguchi, executive vice president of Daiwa, made an estimated 30,000 unauthorized transactions over 11 years resulting in a $1.1 billion loss.

project is a corollary question more often asked of corporate astrologers. This question of Whether is answered by looking at whether the astrological signatures of When, Who, and Where correspond to the intended action. If they do, then go ahead; if they don't, then it's "no go." Of course good CEOs, with the support either of focus groups, computer studies, or executive ESP, will come to the same conclusions as an astrological report—but usually at much greater expense and with a bigger likelihood of error.

How

Finally, the How. This is the true job of the financial astrologer. Like the royal astrologer of times past, he or she can help to coordinate a total systems–planning approach to a business. Depending upon the organization, of course, financial astrologers are still relatively rare, and almost always do their work behind the scenes. They are part of a trusted inner circle of advisers. More and more frequently, however, their advice *is* taken, along with that of accountants and lawyers, as often making a critical difference.

Common to the ancient Babylonians, Chaldeans, Chinese, Egyptians, and Hindus was the preeminent status granted to the astrologer-priest. The astrologer's place in subsequent civilizations has varied from one of honor and prestige to one of mere tolerance and ridicule, or even of heretical criminality.

Yet since the period 1965–1969, and the birth of a New Age awareness in Western society, astrologers have found their work in demand once again. The year 1997 will begin another pivotal period for astrology in general. How come? As an astrologer I would answer: "due to the Uranus–Pluto conjunction in 1965, the Jupiter–Uranus conjunction in 1969, and the upcoming Jupiter–Neptune and Jupiter–Uranus conjunctions in 1997." *Huh?* Explanation to be provided shortly.

Astrology is not only a language but a worldview. I ask simply that you put any prejudices aside for the moment and be open to the *possibility* that the study of astrology is valid. However, I welcome your skepticism. Quite a few of the world's top astrologers were the biggest skeptics—initially. Looking further and deeper into astrology not only may surprise you but, given the real benefits that financial astrology can bring, may become a highly profitable endeavor.

The Three Modern Periods of Financial Astrology

Period 1: The Early Years

While financial astrology has been studied since at least the time of the Babylonians (circa 3000 B.C.), and has played a more or less continuous role in many Asian countries and markets such as Hong Kong, Singapore, and Bombay, most point to the J. P. Morgan hiring of astrologer Evangeline Adams as pivotal and became an open secret on Wall Street. W. D. Gann, one of the legendary futures traders, endorsed astrology as being "the natural law in the markets." In his annual forecast for 1929 he wrote that after September 3 the market would top and would then "experience the biggest crash in its history." Yet in days past astrology was, as today, most often practiced behind the scenes. L. J. Jensen, one of the three original founders of *BusinessWeek,* was an astrologer. Serious tomes on Financial Astrology were few back in the 1930s, with three notable exceptions: Gustave Lambert Brahy's *Key to Forecasting World Events and Economic and Stock Market Cycles,* Louise McWirther's *Astrology and the Stock Market,* and L. J. Jensen's *Astro-cycles and Speculative Markets.*

Period 2: 1987–1992

While many astrologers dabbled in the financial markets in the postwar years, they were largely ignored. Yet many pioneers kept alive the idea that astrology's validity can be shown even in the arena of the financial markets. The pivotal event of course was the prediction of the 1987 crash by a number of financial astrologers including Charles Harvey and Arch Crawford. Immediately some on Wall Street sat up and took notice. Specialized conferences on the role of astrology in the financial markets were organized. Data became more available thanks to researchers such as Carol Mull and Bill Meridian, and specialized computer programs began to appear thanks to the emergence of astrological software houses. On May 2, 1988, The Astrologer's Fund was incorporated to take advantage of these cycles.

One happy result was an increased amount of favorable press coverage. A particular milestone was the invitation extended to this author by *The New York Times* to write an op-ed piece in its business section, the first such invitation ever extended to any astrologer. I was also the first astrologer ever to be written up in *Barron's* for my timely forecasts of the Tokyo market crash. However, most press coverage in this period tended to focus on such sensational incidents as the Gulf War, the minicrash of 1989, and so on. Financial astrology generally obtained media attention only through dire forecasts of impending market disasters. Otherwise it was reserved for unusual New Year forecasts or for such fluff pieces as full-moon or eclipse coverage.

Not until later would the press cover a modest astrological forecast of price movements. This type of forecast had typically been the special prerogative of the "real" prognosticators, i.e., economists and big money managers, presumably on the grounds of "respectability first, then accuracy." Well, who can *really* predict the markets, anyway? As very few financial astrologers managed money at this time, even many of their forecasts tended to be a bit academic and lacking in real-world usefulness.

Period 3: 1993–1997

In February of 1993 the planets Uranus–Neptune conjoined, and the markets became more confused than ever. "Anything goes" is a fair translation of the Uranus–Neptune conjunction. Many markets became even more difficult to predict using the traditional tools, so much so that many more traders started to look to financial astrology for possible guidance, or at least for a second opinion as to confusing market signals.

The first of five annual Astrologers' Fund conferences began on May 17, 1993, in New York City, their goal being to make financial astrology as acceptable as technical analysis. Initial press coverage was bemused.

For example, Andrew Zipser in his *Barron's* preview column of May 8, 1995, wrote:

OUT OF THIS WORLD

What happens if you cross Jeanne Dixon with Peter Lynch? You probably get someone who would attend the stock market forecasting conference hosted by the Astrologers' Fund today and tomorrow at the Hotel Intercontinental. Topics include: "Harmonics of Planetary Periods" and "AstroCycles, the Kinetic Mundascope and Financial Markets." *We aren't making this up.*

Earlier, some press critics had gleefully charged us with gross negligence for booking our first conference at the Vista hotel—a few months *before* terrorists blew it up! My other response to the critics is "I wasn't looking." If an astrologer were to check *every* chart of every person and every event, he or she would have no free time left to *do* anything.

On the other side of the pond, as the *London Times* noted in its front page story of November 20, 1995, that a major "Building Society puts its faith in sky-high Finance...the secret is to forget about consulting Treasury mandates, financial advisors or City economists. We should look instead to 'the oldest source of wisdom in the world' says Abbey National 'the sky itself.' Many of history's wealthiest men and women have had (or still have) a full-time stargazer on their payroll." They offer potential clients a 16-page booklet entitled *Your Astrological Guide to a Secure Future,* offering financial advice for each Zodiac sign. However, they publicly deny that their investment fund managers and actuaries consult the stars when framing their strategy.

Nonetheless, my own plus many other financial astrologers' forecasts continued to pour forth, amazing friends and foes alike. Favorable press coverage increased at an annual rate of over 100 percent during this period. Astrological commentaries began to appear more frequently on radio and TV business shows such as those on CNN and CNBC. Serious—sometimes awestruck—business press coverage also became more frequent. For example, Wall Street astrologer Arch Crawford's *Crawford Perspectives*, an astrology newsletter, was rated No. 1 by many timing-tracking services. Marc Hulbert acknowledged it as one of the top-performing letters of the previous five years. In his *Forbes* column of September 11, 1995, he wrote:

> No, I am not festooning my office wall with astrological charts, nor staying up late nights with the work of Nostradamus. I am only saying that results are what counts, and since results are what Arch Crawford has produced, I will take him seriously—whatever I may think of astrology.

Perhaps another coming-of-age milestone was indicated in a *Forbes* magazine story in its annual Forbes 400 issue of October 16, 1995. This article, entitled, *Which Are the Lucky Stars* professes to be an astrological study of the 400 richest Americans. Unfortunately it is very general, dealing only with Sun Signs. Otherwise it could provide verification of the maxim that success is best achieved by being true to oneself as discussed in Chapter 3. Of more interest in this issue is astrologer Joan Quigley's article referencing Bill Gates and Microsoft. See Chapter 8. Yet, this does demonstrate how astrology is slowly becoming "mainstream" in financial circles. Soon after, *Fortune* ran a similar story.

Another, more compelling example. Astrologer Greg Meadors is the hands-down winner of the *Trader's Catalog and Resource Guide* trading contest. Starting with a hypothetical $50,000 on January 1, 1994, here are the current results as of 1/1/96 (contest runs until 1/97 with Real Time Trading via AUDITRACK simulated funds).

CONTESTANT	START 1/1/94	CURRENT VALUE 1/1/96	PROFITS
Greg Meadors	50,000	$339,651	$289,651
Glenn Neely	50,000	$241,326	$191,326
Third-Best	50,000	$155,791	$105,791

The next two contestants in line had just more than $10,000 profit, while several lost the limit of 100 percent of capital minus $50,000. Yes, futures trading is a highly risky and difficult business. But it's no wonder, with results like these, that more and more futures traders are investigating astrology.

Richard Mogey, director of the Foundation for the Study of Cycles, has become more public about the fact that there is a helpful astrological component to virtually *every* cycle in nature that they have studied. Serious books by experienced market professionals have begun to be published by mainstream houses, as seen in Harper and Row's *Money and the Markets* and this work by McGraw-Hill. *The Wall Street News* has helped to popularize financial astrology on the Internet, compiling the forecasts of a number of financial astrologers. The Astrologers' Fund has opened branded forums on America OnLine and the Microsoft network, and set up its own website on the *International Business Journal* at http://www.ids.net/starbridge/afund.

The Near Future

1997 + Jupiter–Neptune (1/9/97) and Jupiter–Uranus (2/16/97) conjunctions

Forecast: Financial Astrology continuously gains mainstream acceptance, as Wall Street firms and trading houses, as well as corporations worldwide, begin to openly hire financial astrologers. Business news information services such as

Bloomberg, CNBC, CNN, Dow Jones, *Forbes,* and *Fortune* hire astrological columnists and regularly feature financial astrological stories.

In case you're wondering on what grounds I make that prediction, it's simple. All I did really was to translate from astrology into English:

Jupiter = Growth

Uranus = Astrology/Science

Neptune = Astrology/Spirit

Conjunction = Bringing together

That is to say, these aspects "bring together" a "growth" of "astrology" and related "science and spirit" subjects.

Note the last two Jupiter–Uranus conjunction periods—1968–1969, and 1983—and the last two Jupiter–Neptune conjunction periods: 1971 and 1984. Both time periods (1968–1971 and 1983–1984) coincided with great public interest in astrology.

Why Financiers Use Astrologers

The business use of astrology goes far beyond vocational guidance for individuals. Last year, Donald Trump made the news yet again, but this time for a rather different reason: He employed a Feng Shui specialist to inspect a potential building site. In fact, his Hong Kong partners wisely insisted on this. Li Kai Shing, one of the 10 richest men in the world, reportedly pays his astrologer millions of dollars annually. Judging from the results, he may well be getting a great bargain.

Some years ago I had a conversation with the head of the London branch of a large American securities firm who did not believe in astrology and, I dare say, still does not. His point, however, was that someday soon astrology was going to become a factor in the market, simply because so many people *do* believe in it, and inevitably that would influence money flows. It is doing so already, to the tune of many billions of dollars.

In 1992, I was advising a Merrill Lynch broker on a series of currency options. We expected a major move on a given Friday. On Thursday he told me about a conversation he had just had with another broker on his floor, who said that *his* client's astrologer was of an opposite opinion. The fact that I turned out to be right is not the point here. What was interesting to me at the time was that this conversation took place at Merrill Lynch's world headquarters. I knew then that astrology was slowly beginning to come out of the closet.

Some years ago, Credit Lyonnais first published a Chinese astrology forecast of the Hong Kong stock market, as a spoof. It turned out to be dead-on accurate. The cynic's explanation is that this was a self-fulfilling prophecy. Because so many Chinese believe in astrology, it is understandable that many bought and sold according to an astrological forecast. Yet this line of reasoning is in fact faulty, in that it doesn't explain away many other forecasts such as those in the currency markets, where financial astrologers influence only a few billion dollars—often a mere drop in the bucket, as the central bankers have learned.

It has been said that Wall Street tycoons would consult a caged gorilla in the Central Park Zoo if they believed it could forecast the markets with reasonable reliability. I have been in national trading contests against not only some of Wall Street's finest but monkeys, chickens, and (soon) sexily clad dart throwers. Never, however, against a caged gorilla.

My point here is that the gorilla-consulter is interested only in immediate *results* rather than methodology, and that this reveals one striking difference between successful and *very* successful individuals. The latter *generally* are more open to experimentation, and not as deterred by conventional wisdom and prejudices. "Millionaires don't use astrology, billionaires do," a common saying among financial astrologers, has been ascribed to J. P. Morgan. I don't know if he actually said it, but the point *is* valid. Perhaps this is why so many high financiers use astrology: They were simply willing to try it, and they found that it works.

Recently a Hong Kong astrologer began to advertise in *The Economist* a variation on this theme. It went something like:

"Anyone can be a millionaire, but if you want to be *really* rich, use astrology." Personally, I'm not sure that's true. For instance, I'm certain that neither Warren Buffet nor Bill Gates made their money that way. Yet Chinese astrologers do possess a very long and rich tradition, and one entailing the highest and strictest standards. In the ancient imperial court of China, for example, the failure of the royal astrologer to correctly predict an eclipse resulted in *immediate* beheading. Personally, the worst I have suffered for a bad forecast is the loss of a client.

Financial Astrology Is a Dual Specialty

Astrologers as a group are inclined to believe they can do anything. After all, we have the power of the universe behind us; or if we are not so metaphysically inclined, at least we can forecast the future. It is important for the reader to understand that performance as a financial astrologer is based on the command of *both* disciplines.

The reporter who first wrote about me in *Barron's* wondered how it could be that, with my incredible call record, I wasn't making a fortune. There were several reasons for this. First, calling the market is a very different skill from actively trading in it. This is one reason why not all financial astrologers are rich. People vary in their emotional attitude toward money, and this in turn affects their ability to make money.

Prophet or Profit?

Every experienced market participant will tell you that money management is the most important skill. I agree. When I first began to trade in the markets, I would shout with glee "I'm right, I'm right!" (Remember, I *am* a Leo. One reason we Leos like to trade in the markets is that we get to be right every day, or so we believe.) My Taurus associate would then ask: "Did you make money?" Often I would have to reply "No." For example, I might have bought a far-out-of-the-money put (it was cheap), and even though the market would drop 40 points I got virtually nowhere.

I later learned that this isn't an uncommon experience among neophyte traders. Astrologers are especially prone to what some call "learning how to profit from being a prophet." Those of you who are experienced market players know what I mean. If you don't, take some time to learn about investing and trading in a risk-free environment. If some kind soul had just advised me to stick to play money and a Wall Street board game, it would have saved me $38,000. Alternatively, you can work with an experienced financial professional. Remember, it isn't only what you know and when you know, but *how you use it* that counts—whether in the business world or in the markets.

There is also another side to this. I remember well how, some years ago, a neophyte financial astrologer visited me at the New York Astrology Center. He brazenly forecast that on the next weekend there would be a major earthquake in California. He then told me how he had diligently researched those insurance companies with the largest property exposures there, and would short them on Friday afternoon. I remember myself thinking, "My God, can you imagine if he were right? Would he exclaim: 'Hooray, a major earthquake, 10,000 people killed, I'm rich, I'm rich!'?" *Yuck!* Well, there *was* a major earthquake that weekend. Early Monday morning his stocks dropped, but by the end of the day they had risen. Why? There was "only" a billion dollars' worth of damage, and analysts reasoned that this provided the insurance companies with a great excuse to raise premiums! Had this fellow understood markets better, he might not have lost his money.

Another case in point, and a good proof of the old maxim that "What goes around comes around." I had been holier than thou in the preceding case, but when it came to the Gulf War, which I forecast more than two years in advance—mea culpa. I was right in December and early January, when everyone said the war wouldn't happen; we called for a 1200 SP drop on January 9 and also issued a five-star *buy* on oil (our system runs from one to three stars). Everyone laughed until negotiations broke down irrevocably sometime after 1 P.M., when Secretary of State Baker walked out of the negotiating room in Switzerland muttering something to the effect: "I can't talk to that man." Suddenly there were *no* buyers of stock on the exchange. Wonder why?

Now if you remember trading at that time, most people who believed there would be no war were long, and conversely most who believed that war was imminent were short. It turned out there was a war, but such an "easy" war that the universe perversely rewarded those who had forecast wrongly. I was short. Here we were rooting for the war—"Yeah, bomb them...make my day...make me money"—and what happened? The market rallied like crazy the next day! Fortunately, my trading partner was an experienced trader. My forecast was "War in four hours [it was eight], extreme volatility, 85 percent down market, 15 percent up market." If it hadn't been for the money management skills of my partner, who expertly played on the volatility I had predicted, we could have lost a large part of the substantial profits we had accrued over the previous month.

Moral of story: If you trade markets, be a trader. It takes one to two years to learn all the basics. To best use astrology, study astrology. It takes one to three years to learn all the basics. Both are lifelong studies. If you can't be both, work with someone who has the required complementary skills.

It is an obvious point that all financial astrologers are *not* equal in skill, ability, and experience. This fact also accounts for the previously stated observation that not all professional astrologers are rich. Even financial astrologers are not regularly reputed to travel in private jets and own Rolls-Royces. (My recent bride is doing her best to change this markedly unhappy situation!)

Still, there are two more reasons why all astrologers are not rich—and this line of reasoning is the essence of financial astrology. First, *it takes money to make money.* Only recently have astrologers begun to manage and influence large sums of money. Currently, over $14,000,000,000 in the United States and Europe follow the stars. This is the sum total being tracked by money managers and traders whom I know of who utilize the tools of financial astrology. Of course the actual total must be much higher. In addition, if one includes India, Singapore, Hong Kong, and much of Asia, where astrology has traditionally been granted wider cultural acceptance, the figure becomes—dare I say it?—truly *astronomical.*

The second reason relates to the astrological maxim: *You get only what is promised in the natal [birth] chart.* That is also why a poor (not wealthy) astrologer is not necessarily a "poor" astrologer. If you were not born with the potential to be rich, you will not be rich. If you are a broker, you know what I mean from experience. You know why, when you give the identical market advice to four clients, one follows your advice and makes money, another panics if there is a temporary setback and loses money, a third takes a small profit and runs, and a fourth double ups and wins big. Temperament, emotions, psychology, do you say? Remember that astrology *charts* emotions, because as we now know, it is a mathematical psychology based on astronomy.

Financial astrology correlates with all known market mechanisms.

Of the five major potentially knowable factors that influence markets—Fundamental Analysis, Technical Analysis, Market Timing, Market Psychology, and Geopolitical Events—astrological input is necessary for calculating and successfully forecasting *all* five.

Market mechanism	Astrology helpful	Astrology critical
Fundamental Analysis	Yes	No
Technical Analysis	Yes	No
Market Timing	Yes	Yes
Market Psychology	Yes	Yes
Geopolitical Events	Yes	Yes

Whether it is to help them chart cycles and overall market trends, discover pivotal time/price market shifts, select hot stocks, or just be less surprised by the markets, more and more financiers are looking up to the heavens for guidance. How is it done? Enroll in Financial Astrology 101, by reading the next chapter.

Financial Astrology 101

Bull market or bear market?

Buy growth stocks or cyclical stocks?

Buy tech stocks or sell tech stocks?

Wouldn't it be nice to trade in the financial markets with *tomorrow's* newspaper in hand? It would be so simple to answer questions about the market that way, not to mention how much more profitable your portfolio could become. As an alternative to tomorrow's newspaper, Financial Astrology sure is a good forecasting tool, if not quite as foolproof a one. I view astrology as being one of the three "screens" or "layers" requisite for a successful investment strategy. The other two: Fundamental Analysis and Technical Analysis. Ignore Financial Astrology, and you may miss a third or more of the market.

The Three Layers of Stock Market Dynamics

Here they are:

Layer One: Fundamental Analysis

Layer Two: Technical Analysis

Layer Three: Financial Astrology

Imagine for a moment that you are consulting for a large Wall Street trading house. Someone in the firm has been tracking the forecasts of a number of financial astrologers, and sometimes she finds them to be "like reading the financial section of tomorrow's newspaper." You have been hired to run a pilot study of whether astrology has any real value when it comes to investing and trading in the financial markets. To begin with, you find that you have basically two choices.

Choice #1 is to *match astrology with the markets,* to first find a database of significant astrological events and then correlate them to any perceived market events such as top, bottom, change of trend, and so forth. Choice #2 is to *match market action with astrology,* to analyze a database of significant market events such as the 100 best or worst days of the markets or the rise/crash of a superstock and then see what, if any, astrological features are present. Assuming that you find some correlation, you then will attempt to make some tentative market forecasts based upon what you have found. If the results of these forecasts are encouraging you will look further into the subject; if not, it's back to chaos theory, neural networks, and artificial intelligence.

Let's now say that you decide arbitrarily to take the first course of action. You decide that in order to proceed, you will first have to gain some understanding of the fundamentals of astrology before you can begin to apply them to the financial markets. You visit your local bookstore and purchase a copy of *Investing by the Stars.* What do you find?

Briefly, financial astrology first indicates the *natal* or *basic* nature of a stock or stock market. By comparing the state of the current heavens to a company or stock market's birth data, one can astrologically chart and forecast the company or market's changing fortunes.

Pattern recognition is the basis for any forecast of When and How Fast stock prices will change. For instance:

Stock #1 UP	Pattern B1, B2, B3...
Stock #1 DOWN	Pattern S1, S2, S3...
Stock #2 UP	Pattern B1, B2, B3...
Stock #2 DOWN	Pattern S1, S2, S3...
Stock #3 UP	Pattern B1, B2, B3...
Stock #3 DOWN	Pattern S1, S2, S3...

We discover similar patterns when companies become highly profitable. We find similar but also different patterns, when companies lose money or go bankrupt. Many economic cycles have astrological signatures, and correspond in part to planetary cycles. So too, bull markets and bear markets have astrological correspondences. Some of these patterns are simple and easy to recognize, yet many more are quite complex and hard to discern. In addition, real-life markets are quite challenging and astrological forecasting is not as easy in practice as in theory. Nonetheless, the use of astrology *can* and *does* help one to anticipate both market trends and stock-price movements. Given today's frenzied trading world, I have often felt that I might have become a heavy drinker *if* I hadn't had a horoscope to guide me through so many difficult and volatile market trading days.

We must always remember that astrology is itself an observational science. Therefore, when we apply financial astrological theory to the markets, the ultimate arbiter of truth here remains the market itself. Theories that don't fit facts must be revised or out-and-out abandoned.

Key Concepts

Astrologers are trained to look to the sky for guidance. The sky at birth or natal birth chart indicates potential, while the positions of the planets in the sky at any given moment, called transits, indicate the likely course of present and future events.

SKY AT BIRTH = NATAL BIRTH CHART

SKY TODAY = TRANSITS

The *natal horoscope* or birth chart refers to the birth moment itself. For a company it is the time, place, and date of incorporation that is used. (See Fig. 2-1 for an example.)

It is also important to chart the *first trade* horoscope of a company (on its stock exchange). (See Figs. 2-2 and 2-3 for example.) Financial astrologers may also refer to many other

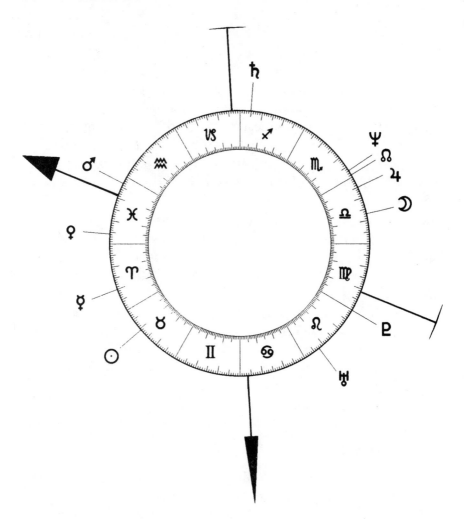

FIGURE 2-1   Incorporation chart of IBM.

horoscopes as well. These include those of different countries, stock markets, and central banks, in addition to those of their clients and financial advisers. A plethora of charts to look at, indeed.

The birth moment is highly important, as it *defines* the potential manifestation of the entity as well as its possible/probable manifestation in time. For a person it shows the strengths and potential weaknesses associated with character, talent, and ability. For a company it shows how successful it will be in

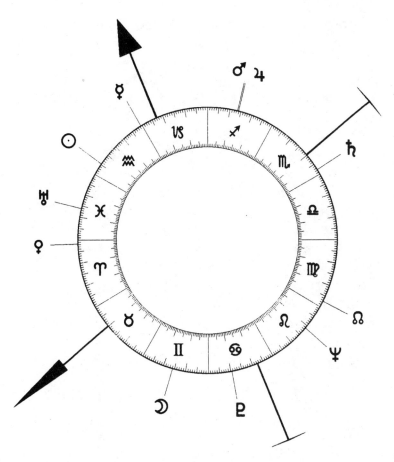

FIGURE 2-2   First trade chart of IBM.

its chosen industry, and when. The birth chart is subject to analysis by dozens of timing techniques that astrologers have used for centuries such as Transits, Progres-sions, Directions, Solar and Lunar Returns, and Dasa or Planetary periods, to name just a few.

The term *transit* refers to the current placement of the planets. Roughly speaking, if you were to look up at the sky and record what you see, it would be the transiting planets, i.e., the current state of the sky. It is their constantly changing relationship to the natal horoscope chart that is the basis of almost all astrological prediction.

Financial astrologers not trained in classical astrological

theory generally stop here. Some indeed don't even use the birth charts of stocks or markets but solely the transits of the planets to help them identify and forecast significant market turning points. But such financial astrologers who use *only* transits, the current state of the heavens, find that in many instances an astrological event (transit) occurs *without* causing any noticeable market effect. On the other hand, *every* major event in the market *is* correlated to a major planetary event. Therefore many believe a wise astrological approach to the markets always *begins* with technical analysis.

For financial astrologers like myself, however, transits are only one tool in our toolbox, albeit a very handy and crucial one. Transits *time* events, much like the hands of a clock. They may be looked upon as only one *key trigger* of basic natal potentiality, whereas a number of interlocking factors must be present to precipitate any given event or market activity.

Put another way, transiting planets activating the natal planets represents a *necessary* but not a *sufficient* cause of stock and stock market action. When used in conjunction with those other astrological predictive techniques mentioned previously, they act as a timer or trigger. Using a classical triple-trading-screen model, the natal planets, directed planets, and transits would be one screen, and the natal planets, progressed planets, and transits and so forth, another.

Don't expect to take all of this in at once. As we go further and present examples, it will begin to make sense. For the moment, keep in mind that astrologers look to the planets of our solar systems as *timers*. The primary technique used is called transits, which indicates the relationship of the current state of the heavens to the natal or initial state. Astrologers look to special patterns of this relationship to forecast positive and negative market trends.

FINANCIAL ASTROLOGY TECHNIQUE	USE
Transits only	Market timing
Transits and natal state	Stock and market timing
Transits and natal state and more	Stock and market timing

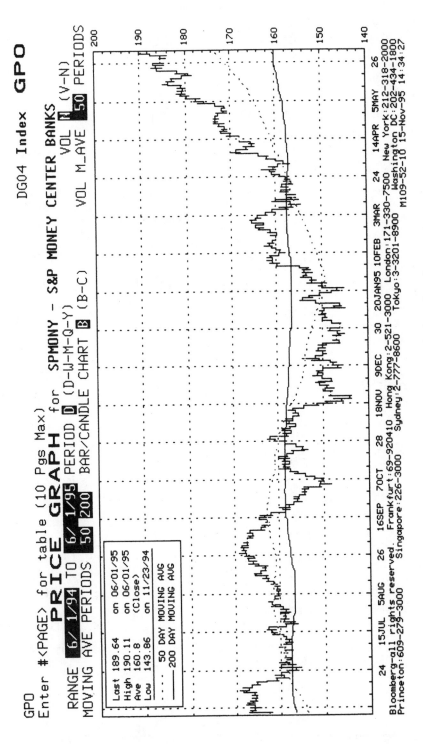

FIGURE 2-3 One-year S&P money center bank chart. (*Courtesy of Bloomberg.*)

The primary business planets are Jupiter and Saturn. In general this planetary pair represents the expansion (Jupiter) and contraction (Saturn) of the business cycle. In times of excess we have the dynamics of greed (Jupiter) and fear (Saturn). The basic condition of a market is an up (Jupiter) or down (Saturn) movement. There are exceptions, as to any rule, but first let's get some of the basics down before we worry about those.

	JUPITER	SATURN
Principle	Expansion	Contraction
Psychology	Optimism	Pessimism
Extreme	Greed	Fear
Market Action	Up	Down

Let us also consider one well-known fact of astrological rulership: that Jupiter "rules" (i.e., correlates to) the banking industry. What happens when Jupiter conjuncted (is together with) Pluto, as it did in December of 1994? Did this time period correspond to an upturn in banking stocks? It did.

Note: One of Pluto's effects is to exaggerate the effect of a planet it contacts. The keyword used by astrologers is *super,* hence the outperformance by banking stocks during this period. How very nice. Let's try another simple example as a test.

Traditionally the sign Leo is said to rule gold, while Cancer rules silver. But does gold go up with Jupiter in Leo, or silver with Jupiter in Cancer? Conversely, does gold go down with Saturn in Leo, or silver with Saturn in Cancer? Tradition might suggest that they do, but the gold and silver markets don't fully agree. Astrological practice isn't that easy and simple, neither in the gold and silver markets nor, unfortunately, in *any* market. One major reason for the complexity is that we are not dealing with just two planets.

I will try not to be over-technical in the discussion that follows. It is important only to identify the principles, not to memorize the details. After a few repeated exposures, the details will become obvious to you. At this time I simply want you to appreciate some of the complexity as well as the elegance of astrological theory.

Because there are only nine planets (plus a few asteroids and a number of moons) in our solar system, there is a lot of multiple assignment of rulerships to each planet. In order to arrive at a specific correspondence we use a combination of planets called *aspects*. Taking Jupiter as an example, we consider not merely Jupiter by itself but also its relationships with all the other planets. This reiterates up to a total of *four levels*. Taking just one of the combinations, that of Jupiter with Neptune, this is once again subject to association with each of the nine planets. If we associate Jupiter–Neptune with Pluto as one instance, this is once more subject to nine-plus possible combinations. If we take its association with Uranus, we have one significator of lotteries and the gaming industry.[*] This complexity allows for an extremely large collection of objects, all based on a relatively few principles. Thousands of rulerships or correspondences can be assigned to a combination of the 10 planetary principles. (Astrologers use the Sun and Moon plus eight planets—no Earth.) Once a principle has been established it can then be correlated to any holistic system, whether a person, company, or stock. Wow!

Planetary "Rulership" of Stocks and Commodities

According to the doctrine of signatures, each planet in astrology has rulership over various spheres. In ancient times, Mars was the god of war, and today it retains the same association with violence. Modern counseling astrologers tend to be psychological in their orientation, speaking of the "energies" and "functions" associated with the planets. Mars represents the

---

*To the astrologically literate, one principle of Jupiter is wealth. Using a keyword definition found in many elementary textbooks, here are some astrological definitions: Jupiter–Uranus = Quick Money; Jupiter–Neptune = Easy Money; and Jupiter–Pluto = Money in Time. With this knowledge in hand, Jupiter's relationship to speculation makes sense.

principle of self-assertion, indicating our relative tendency to aggressiveness, in extreme cases to violence. Yet in financial astrology we generally restrict our discussion to objects, e.g., companies, and to literal events. Thus when we refer to the planet Mars we are thinking about the steel or war/defense industries. The following are a few examples of classical rulerships:

Sun	Precious metals
Moon	Health care, household products, restaurants
Mercury	Telecoms, media, transportation
Venus	Apparel, cosmetics, recreation, retailers
Mars	Sports, steel, defense, industrial machinery
Jupiter	Banking, brokerage and financial services
Saturn	Agriculture, real estate
Uranus	Astrology, computers and technology, aerospace
Neptune	Entertainment, chemicals, pharmaceuticals
Pluto	Mineral resources

For astrologers, of course, many industries share more than one rulership. For instance, telecommunications is best described as Uranus (Tele) plus Mercury (Communication). Advertising is best described as Moon (public), Mercury (Communication), and Pluto (manipulation). Also, a number of rulerships currently assigned to Uranus, Neptune, and Pluto were historically assigned to the seven planets visible to the naked eye. Thus mining was said by ancient and medieval astrologers to be ruled by Saturn. Likewise one could theoretically argue whether casinos are ruled by Jupiter or Neptune, oil companies by Neptune or Pluto (oil *drilling* clearly is Pluto). Please refer to the basic astrology textbooks listed in Appendix IV. The important point to note here is that rulerships or correlations can be assigned to various stocks or industry groups, which can then be made the subject of testing.

The prediction of crop production, or the lack of it, has a long history among astrologers. Agriculture was of course vital to all early civilizations, from the early Egyptians and Babylonians on. Albiruni's textbook *The Elements of Astrology* was the classic textbook of Arabic astrology in the middle ages. It is noteworthy for many reasons. One reason the book was noteworthy was his list of 24 Lots, or Arabic points, to prognosticate crops:

1.	Wheat	Sun, Jupiter
2.	Barley, meat	Moon, Jupiter
3.	Rice, millet	Jupiter, Venus
4.	Maize	Jupiter, Saturn
5.	Pulse	Venus, Mercury
6.	Lentils and iron	Mars, Saturn
7.	Beans, onions	Saturn, Mars
8.	Chickpeas	Venus, Sun
9.	Sesame, grapes	Saturn, Venus
10.	Sugar	Venus, Mercury
11.	Honey	Moon, Sun
12.	Oil	Mars, Moon
13.	Nuts, flax	Mars, Venus
14.	Olives	Mercury, Moon
15.	Apricots	Saturn, Mars
16.	Watermelons	Jupiter, Mercury
17.	Salt	Moon, Mars
18.	Sweets	Sun, Venus
19.	Astringent	Mercury, Saturn
20.	Pungent things	Mars, Saturn
21.	Raw silk, cotton	Mercury, Venus
22.	Purgatives	Mercury, Saturn
23.	Bitter purgatives	Saturn, Mars
24.	Acid purgatives	Saturn, Jupiter

It's time now to enunciate the three core principles, and then the three basic rules, of financial astrology. Each of the later chapters will demonstrate their application. Again, don't be concerned with memorizing them, just try to get a "feel" for them. They will be applied and reapplied throughout the book.

The Three Core Principles

The first core principle of astrological investing is Theme Investing. This theme we select with the greatest of care—indeed, with heavenly guidance.

The second core principle of astrological investing is Timing. This is why "Be there first!" is the motto of the Astrologers' Fund.

The third core principle of astrological investing is Place. Astrology maps the effects of the planets both in time and in space. This is why this book could be subtitled "An Astrological Guide to the Global Markets."

The Three Rules of Financial Astrology

Rule #1: You Get Only What Is Promised in Your Natal Chart

This rule can be applied in a variety of areas. From IPOs who want to be the next Microsoft, to forecasting the expected success of a company's expansion into new markets, to whether it is wise for an ordinary conservative investor to try to make a killing in the futures markets. Life is full of uncertainty and risk, but when we ignore astrology I believe we increase our chances of encountering a market disaster *by definition: dis* means "away," *astres* "the stars."

Rule #2: Big Moves and Events Call for Big Indicators

Rule #3: One Indication Is a Possibility, Two Are a Probability, Three Are a Certainty

We are referring here to multiple horoscope indications, as any major event will show up not only with big indicators but with multiple indicators. These indicators can come from within astrology itself or from the correlation of astrological to technical and fundamental factors.

Cross-market Confirmation and Family Horoscopes

The more one trades the markets, the more respect one develops for them. One sure sign of a beginner is his or her "I can do anything!" attitude. Another is taking it personally: "The market owes *me*!" or "Today I will *beat* the market!" Therefore before placing large bets—or should I have said, making a major investment—one requires a reasonable amount of confirmation. Unfortunately, in the case of many technical timing indicators, by the time sufficient confirmation has been obtained it may be too late to catch the major move, and one will be left with only table scraps. Too many trend-following techniques suffer from this deficiency. Thus we all must learn to balance risks and rewards. Naturally we all wish to *maximize* reward and *minimize* risk! One key way to do this is through cross-market confirmation.

For example if one is trading the gold market—a personal favorite of mine—one looks to find an integrated scenario of interest rates, world stability/instability, and, currently, a generally inverse correlation to the dollar (since the Gulf War, the historic relation of gold to the dollar and to world crises has broken down). One also follows the XAU (Gold-Silver Index) which is a leading indictor of gold prices, and the horoscopes of individual gold stocks. One can also look to the horoscope of the New York Commodity Exchange, COMEX. All of the above (and more) should be relatively in sync before one makes a major gold move.

This is called "the family horoscope phenomenon." For example if a spouse dies, it will show up not only in the spouse's chart but also in the children's charts. Similarly, a major gold move will show up in various gold stocks and global gold markets. We will talk more about this principle under Markets, as it is a very vital one.

Rulerships Change

Just as the nature of the markets changes, so do astrological rulerships or correspondences. Consider the airplane industry. Initially astrologers said it was ruled by the planet Uranus. More recently they have considered it to be "ruled" by the planet Neptune. Why? Let's suspend our super-rational thinking processes for a moment, and save them to test our tentative conclusions.

The doctrine of signatures or correspondences tells us to look for alignment of similarity—for the highest degree of analogy, so to speak. Initially, aviation was very much a seat-of-the-pants, daredevil activity, very akin to the typical Uranian personality as seen by modern astrology. Today, however, the flying of modern aircraft is a much more civilized experience, no longer the adventure it once was. This allows flying's essential nature to emerge. What is that nature? *To get high!* In astrology that function is ruled by Neptune. So how about a real-live test? Putting our money where our mouth is, and taking *no* chances, we picked Boeing stock as one of the choices in a recent long-term trading contest. As we approach 1997 and the Jupiter–Uranus and Jupiter–Neptune conjunctions, given either rulership, traditional or modern, Boeing will outperform the market.

Similarly, reinforcement or intersection theory tells us that whether the gaming/casino industry is ruled or coruled by Jupiter or Neptune, it will show strong growth at least into the Jupiter–Neptune conjunction of 1997. This should come as no surprise to most market analysts, though. Remember that the Truth is the truth, and can often be seen by non-astrological means. Sometimes it's obvious to all, sometimes not.

Dow Jones Industrial Average

As we all well know, "rules" not only have exceptions but also are subject to change. When I first started studying the market in late 1987, the NYSE market never moved without IBM.

(Interestingly if we compare the horoscope of IBM with that of the NYSE we can see the reasons for this. They both have a strong Taurus influence, for example.) Yet within a few short years, IBM fell from grace as the DJIA bellwether. My mentor who taught me this rule hasn't mentioned it in many years, and may even have forgotten about it. Today GE, GM, and Exxon are perhaps the best bellwether DJIA stocks, but I don't know anyone who uses them in a fashion similar to the old IBM rule.

We have already mentioned that markets change. This is due largely to two factors: the rise of the mutual funds, and the enormous rise in the use of derivatives and the futures markets. Then too, the vastly increased power and use of computers act to compress traditional cycle lengths. A stock correction of, say, 20 percent, which might have taken months to play itself out in previous times, can now occur rapidly over a period of days. But I am sure you knew I would say that astrology is another major factor. We will see for example that the reunification date of Germany at midnight of October 3, 1990, forever changed the German national chart. This is not as strange as it sounds. This event also changed the psyche of the people, who once again were citizens of a whole country.

Timers tend to keep a close eye on seasonality—the effect of the summer growing season on the grain market being an obvious example. But one must also consider the monthly, quarterly, and year-end cycles, as investment managers are increasingly compensated by market performance at the end of each of these, and look to the effect of year-end tax calendar issues—April 15 in U.S. markets or April 1 in the Japanese market. Astrologers seek to chart these moments, believing that the cosmic condition at the beginning of each cycle is indicative of the cycle's character. Financial astrologers celebrate solstices and equinoxes in much the same way as individuals do their birthdays. By the way, birthdays are astrologically very important times, and portend much of the ensuing year's possibilities. This is why it is generally good advice to joyously celebrate one's birthday, as it helps to set a quality tone for the upcoming year.

Other market cycles to be watched closely are the so-called January effect in small-cap stocks; the Summer Rally; the October Crash, aka the Fall's Fall; the Santa Claus Rally, etc. Today, especially since the Uranus–Neptune conjunction of 1993, astrologers are being called upon to predict answers to questions as seemingly odd as "Who's buried in Grant's Tomb?" The market equivalent is "In which month will the January effect take place: late November, December, January, or early February?"

The following are some sample astrological cycles.

SHORT-TERM CYCLES	AVERAGE LENGTH
Daily rotation	Daily
Lunar	Monthly

INTERMEDIATE-TERM CYCLES	AVERAGE LENGTH
Mercury	88 days
Venus	225 days

LONG-TERM CYCLES	AVERAGE LENGTH
Jupiter	12 years
Jupiter–Saturn	20 years
Nodal cycles	19 years

The single-planet cycles that have been compiled have different lengths according to whether they are geocentric (earth-centered) or heliocentric (sun-centered), and other variables. The relevance to the markets of still more complex or combined planetary cycles is beyond the scope of this introductory work.

More important than fixed-length cycles in economics are the irregular cycles tied to planetary movement. Planetary cycles perhaps just mark time like the hands of a clock, although probably with some effect. Yet there are numerous astronomical cycles that have astrological significance, such as the daily rotation cycles, monthly and yearly soli-lunar cycles, and the 12- and 60-year Jupiter cycles. We can also find planetary correlations to sunspot cycles, which in turn correlate to economic cycles. All of these cycles give us merely a hint of the major overall effect astrology can have on the markets.

Dozens of more technical factors also come into play in financial astrology, and a number of them will be covered in subsequent chapters. All are integrated with a variety of timing-indicator factors in both geocentric and heliocentric reference frames. Both seem to have validity.

Astrology and Triple-screen Investing

The idea that a particular possibility shows up across systems is one solid approach to astrological investing. For long-term investing, the *ideal* is an investment that meets fundamental, technical, *and* astrological criteria. Because it is our view that the astrological is equal in importance to the technical and the fundamental, the nonapplication of astrology to finance results in at least one-third of market dynamics not being adequately accounted for.

Conversely, however, if astrologers were to ignore the fundamental and the technical, they would be missing out on two-thirds of market dynamics.

Unique Events versus Cyclic Patterns

Most financial astrologers have tended to concentrate on market cycles. There are many reasons for this, but the primary one is that investing/trading against a major cycle is like motorboating against a strong wind: You may still reach your goal, but the cost in fuel (money) will be far higher than if you had gone with the flow. Another, perhaps, is that a higher level of training and experience is called for if unique market events are to be successfully forecast. Yet commensurate with the extra effort is the extra reward.

It is obvious that major events show up with major indicators. These indicators are of course shown in astrology, but in other technical systems as well. You can use any combination of techniques that you find to be consistently reliable. Hopefully they will be sufficiently good advance indicators to be profitable. Astrologers have no monopoly on the truth, although I strongly believe we often get first dibs!

Two Theoretical Approaches to Forecasting

The first theoretical approach is that of exact mathematical space (Saturn). This maintains that it is possible to chart *each* moment of time, from the largest time periods imaginable down to the smallest. In Indian astrology these periods range from a Yuga cycle of 432,000 years down to the average length of an individual breath or heartbeat. (Such potential precision is however beyond the grasp of *this* practitioner, using the techniques readily available in the public domain.) The financial astrological forecasters who subscribe to this theory try to forecast every day's action in all of the markets, and I believe this results in far too many errors in practice.

The second approach is that of guidepost theory (Neptune), and I employ this more free-form type of market forecasting. In other words, I use astrology in order to gain advance notification of many *definite* symbolic events, then build various scenarios around them. I prefer to notate those times that are most strongly indicated. If they are seconded by other indicators, all the better, but a sufficiently robust astrological indicator will almost always "manifest." These definite markers or time periods have value both for long-term investing and for short-term trading horizons.

Three Methods of Approach

The integration of astrology with conventional market analysis is done by using financial astrology as

1. A primary tool
2. A second opinion
3. A blackboard model input

While financial astrology can be used in a stand-alone mode, most readers will benefit by simply adding it to their time and price systems, ideally to create a "triple-screen" method. Stock market analysts generally look to a few simple tools to enhance their current methodology, while those grounded in astrological practice naturally tend to use more and more varied astrological techniques.

Financial Astrology as a Primary Tool

We do not see astrology as being a magic bullet, or an instant passport to riches. Nonetheless, the depth and variety of astrological tools is amazing. Whether it is used as a microscope in day trading or a telescope in forecasting long-range market shifts, astrology has something to offer every market participant.

Astrology is of great use in helping one to select both the What and the When, but additional technical and fundamental tools can be used to confirm one's choices. Very few financial astrologers use *only* astrological tools to forecast markets, and most likely these are the beginners. Of course if the indicators are extremely strong no confirmation may be required, especially if it is a market "surprise" that is anticipated.

Financial Astrology as a Second Opinion

Most successful fund managers who study astrology do so after first developing a trading and investing style that has gone on to prove itself a success. Not looking to replace existing tools and techniques, they wish to augment them. Initially pleasantly surprised by what astrology can do for them, they soon come to take it for granted. Yet if both astrology and their worldview agree, they are much more likely to make money than when divergences exist. It is prudent money management to seek confirmation from astrology.

Of course, if a money manager were to use financial astrology not as a second opinion but as a first, he/she could become the object of a legal suit, especially if it were not fully disclosed in advance to the clients. Nonetheless, most financiers who make use of astrology are still in the closet. They may not see any economic advantage in proclaiming the virtues of it, as they have no desire to give away their best secrets and possibly be sued in the bargain.

Financial Astrology as a Blackboard Model Input

In this third technique, multiple independent knowledge sources, which can include more than one astrological forecasting system, are combined *together* to paint a more complete picture than any single forecaster or forecasting system could do. It is analogous to a "team of experts" approach, whereby each person communicates his or her expertise to a group leader/facilitator, who then feeds back to the group any new market conditions and decisions taken. This approach to market forecasting and trading is highly computerized, and currently highly secret. Theoretically at least, it can provide the highest degree of accuracy and precision in market modeling.

Now let's do a quick recap of the five principal factors in astrological trading or investing, the Who, What, Where, When, and How.

Who

The first rule of financial astrology is to *look to your own chart for guidance*. This encompasses not only the psychology of the trader/investor but is our recommended starting point for all subsequent studies in financial astrology.

What

Looking first at planetary themes, we choose *what* kinds of investments and trades to make. Then we look to the horoscopes of the individual stocks we wish to buy/sell, as the natural second step in financial astrological analysis.

Where

Looking at mundane horoscopes (primarily those of countries and markets), we decide where we will invest our money.

When

Again we look to each of the above horoscopes to determine *when* is the best time to buy/sell.

How

This is where the cospecialty aspect of financial astrology comes in. It bears repeating that it is not only what you know but *how* you use it that counts in the markets. Choosing the best instruments to play is a vastly important skill in itself. This is important not only in trading but applies to investing as well. If you don't know when it's advantageous to buy preferred over common stock, or what markets are best for convertible bonds versus stocks, or what asset allocation is, you're probably playing the Wall Street game like an amateur. You may be lucky and win, even when you're up against pros with skill, knowledge, and experience, but don't kid yourself that you're on a level playing field. Rather than risk losing your shirt, you can either choose to spend the time it will take to learn or else work with a financial professional, preferably one with an openness to, or some knowledge of, financial astrology.

Know Thyself

Three primary uses of financial astrology involve:

1. *Style:* Finding one's investing comfort level from one's horoscope
2. *Timing:* When to go for the brass ring, when to take a vacation
3. *Synastry:* Choosing one's financial adviser, trading partner(s), and markets

The first rule of financial astrology is to look to your *own* horoscope for guidance. One common denominator of successful traders and investors is that each expresses his or her own *unique* style. Astrology helps one to discover one's own personal trading/investing style, market affinities, and timing cycles. I have previously mentioned the astrological maxim "You get only what is promised in the natal chart." By being "true to oneself" one certainly promotes great personal happiness, but what about the bottom line? Does inner honesty automatically lead to greater profitability? Is success really "written in the stars"?

First, a slight digression. As we were going to press, *Forbes* magazine was doing a sun sign study of the 400 richest Americans. This shows not only that astrology is slowly becoming "mainstream" in financial circles, but also provides verification of the maxim that success is best achieved by being true to oneself.

If the Shoe Fits, Wear It

Even if you are without the benefit of seeing an astrologer, you can consciously align yourself with an investment style. Do you prefer growth or value? Short-term trading or long-term investing? Do you prefer to purchase a stock because of strong fundamentals or a good technical chart? Do you "consider the trend your friend," or do you prefer to be a contrarian?

Most experienced and successful investors have found their own uniquely satisfactory answers to the previous questions. When I first obtain a new client, I ask them to fill out a client profile. (See Appendix III.) Much of this information request is standard, except for the personal astrology data and investing history. Here I ask for their birth time, place, and date, as well as their trading/investing objectives and previous experience(s). I am primarily looking for a *match* between their basic horoscope nature and their business objectives. Where these do not match, or where their past market experiences have been unfortunate, I look to their horoscope to find creative ways of changing their overall investment strategy. Beyond this, I act in a fairly straightforward advisory capacity.

In addition to the important issue of investing style, financial astrologers also look at the very same non-astrological factors any financial consultant would. One primary consideration is risk tolerance. At the one extreme we have the very risk-averse, such as many retirees for whom a steady, safe income is the number-one consideration. At the other extreme we have the aggressive risk-taker, he or she who above all looks for growth of principle as an upwardly mobile young executive might. Broadly speaking, I list my clients under one of two headings: Wealth Preservation, or Wealth Creation.

Clients already in possession of considerable wealth are most concerned with its maintenance, as well as with protection from inflation, excessive taxation, the threat of expropriation of properties, and similar issues. Their investment decisions generally are conservative, and taken from a long-term perspective. Conversely, when wealth creation is the paramount consideration, trading issues dominate investing strategies that are aggressive by nature. Usually this results in more frequent portfolio turnovers, as one feature of the quest for the greatest possible appreciation of principal.

I have in mind here two associates. The first is a consummate day-trader and wealth-creator. When I first started working with him I encountered a severe language problem. He would say, for example, that he was so bullish that he would be "long forever" in the stock market. Two days later I was shocked to learn that he was short the market that day. This happened a few times before I realized that as a day trader his time horizon generally was one day; overnight trading was "long-term," and two days were "forever."

Conversely, another associate and investment banker (and closet financial astrologer), who buys and sells *large* positions, trades only with the secular trend. He can ignore an easily perceptible but countertrend DJIA move of 50+ points, because his trading horizon is generally months and his investment horizon years. Not surprisingly, the current minimum account for my trading friend is $5000, while for my investment banker friend it's $5 million!

Arriving at One's True Comfort Level

Through personal experience I have discovered the great importance of client comfort level. If a client is comfortable with a position, he or she will stick with it even in the face of adversity. If it was simply thrust upon him/her, it is likely to be abandoned all too easily.

There are several dimensions to comfort level. We have already spoken about risk tolerance. In astrology the primary indicators are the planets Mars and Saturn. A person with a strong Mars likes risk, while a strong Saturnian is generally more risk-averse.

A second dimension to comfort level has to do with your own personal view of the economy. If you believe it will be robust, then an investment in an aggressive growth fund may be suitable. If you believe we are headed for a recession, then purchasing a bond portfolio may be the more attractive alternative.

Finally, we look to Venus as the prime astrological significator of comfort. It represents what everybody likes. Astrologers should look to its sign and aspect placement for clues.

When to Sell Stocks

The stock market is a mechanism for the buying and *selling* of stocks. Yet I find that most people spend far too little time pondering What and When to sell. Often they feel that their work has been done once they have determined What and When to buy. That is why I wish to balance the equation by suggesting that you review/evaluate your portfolio each month or quarter.

I have three rules for this process. However, I must point out that I will be leaving the tax consequences of selling to one side, as these are best addressed individually. But in any case, if a stock is clearly headed to the basement it is far better to sell it at once, regardless of its current profit or loss status and the possible tax consequences.

Rule #1: *Sell immediately when you would no longer buy the stock at the current price.* You are assuming that other people are not as smart or perceptive as you if they buy at the current or higher price, and often that's a very dangerous assumption. Alternatively, you can place a close-sell stop.

Rule #2: *Sell immediately the moment you become uncomfortable owning a stock.* For example, if you hold several positions and there is only one that consistently bothers you, *sell it*. Why be uncomfortable? Allow discomfort to intuitively alert you to a future problem, rather than goad you into errors of judgment.

Rule #3: *Sell whenever a stock's horoscope indicates possible trouble ahead.* After all, if we don't follow astrology, why am I writing, and you reading, this book? We may be wrong, but the odds are in our favor. I'll be providing several examples of this in later chapters.

The market is continually providing new opportunities, but

since we don't have unlimited resources we must make choices. Review your asset allocation every quarter if you are an active investor/trader and each year if you are not. Assets traditionally are allocated among cash, bonds, and stocks, and broken down into "income-oriented" and "growth-oriented" portfolios. Other financial planners add a category by including tangible or real assets such as real estate, precious metals, and collectibles. I also separately include commodities, to bring the category total to five.* In a conservative portfolio commodities would be used more for hedging than speculation purposes, or not at all, depending on level of client comfort.

A final issue is that of Diversity versus Concentration. Among trading positions, I personally find my ideal number to be five. For investing purposes, my personal comfort level stipulates that I diversify into no less than 6 and no more than 12 different industries/markets/positions. I can't adequately keep track and be knowledgeable about more than 12. Seek (and find) your own ideal minimum and maximum.

In investing, a million-dollar portfolio is of course allocated differently than a $10,000 one. Take the 5 percent rule, which stipulates that one should never risk more than 5 percent of the portfolio on any single trading position. While this makes perfect sense for big investors, applying it to a $10,000 account—that is, limiting exposure to $500 investing positions—certainly doesn't. Just today, on the Internet, someone asked me "How would you invest $10,000, assuming that is all your assets?" Before answering, I indicated that I needed more information about

The situation of the client: retired, just starting out, married with children?

Future financial prospects: stable, improved, diminished?

Investment objective, and risk tolerance?

---

*There are numerous ways to do asset allocation. Some portfolio managers subdivide each category, such as stocks, into small caps, blue chips, and internationals, or bonds into corporate and government, and so forth.

Of course if this had been my client, I would also have asked for horoscope data. But my point is that you should have/seek lots of answers to lots of questions before you jump in with investment advice.

Planetary Investment Styles

Here are a few sample planetary investing styles for you to peruse. Can you find your own? Of course none of us is just *one* planetary type, and you may have more than one planet that is very strong in your horoscope.

Sun: Industry leaders, blue chips

Moon: Trend-following

Mercury: Day-trading; primary ruler of stocks

Venus: Primary ruler of bonds

Mars: Hot stocks, deals, options; keyword is *action*; contrarian (likes to fight), startups

Jupiter: Growth investing

Saturn: Straight arrow, Value Investing, Shorting

Uranus: IPOs; keyword is *new*

Neptune: Story stocks, rumor plays, venture capital

Pluto: Mergers and acquisitions, turnaround candidates, insider trading

Here are a few combinations of planets:

Venus–Moon: Trend-following, what's popular

Mars–Jupiter: Aggressive growth

Mars–Uranus: Contrarians

Saturn–Pluto: Widows and orphans, turnaround candidates

Mercury–Neptune: Story stocks

Thinking Like an Astrologer

Now let's apply the planets directly to some possible investing styles. Astrologers know that an investor with a strong Mars likes action. He/she is a natural risk-taker who likes to play hot stocks. Alternately, he/she could express this action in playing options, futures, or emerging markets. The Mars type also loves a challenge. In times of excess they are foolhardy— warriors on horseback charging against the cannon! Their greatest nemesis is impatience.

In terms of combining planets, if an investment has both Mars and Jupiter strong, an aggressive growth fund will be appropriate. Strong Neptunians need to be careful to avoid the kind of scams so prevalent in the penny stock market, yet because every coin has two sides, their intuition or native psychic ability can also help them to anticipate trends far into the future—a quality highly valued on Wall Street! This is also a good combination for a venture capitalist, as it allows her or him to foresee possibilities far in advance.

Sun Signs and Investing

I am sure my readers are more familiar with their sun sign than their planetary type. Perhaps it is because I have so vigorously campaigned against sun sign astrology for many years that I tend to overlook the value of these signs in investing. Certainly a strong case can be made for a number of possible correlations, such as between Aries and startup companies, or Virgo and technical analysis. Remember please that your sun sign is just one of several important factors in your horoscope, and that your Moon sign and Mercury and Venus signs also are important. I have included a large referral list of astrologers in Appendix IV, if/when you would like to check out your horoscope personally. The following examples are provided only with the reservations just stated, and reader feedback and experience will be most welcome here.

Aries   Startups
Taurus   Bonds
Gemini   Trading
Cancer   Real estate
Leo   Large caps
Virgo   Technical analysis
Libra   Relationship investing
Scorpio   Hostile takeovers
Sagittarius   International
Capricorn   Blue chips, savings
Aquarius   Contrarian
Pisces   SRI: socially responsible investing

Astrologers also have traditionally assigned certain industry sectors to the signs, such as banking to Taurus or media to Gemini. In theory these should correspond to favorite sectors. We will deal with this topic in Chapter 5.

For demonstration purposes we will now look briefly at the horoscopes of two of the most famous names in investing: Warren Buffet and Peter Lynch.

Peter Lynch is perhaps the best-known apostle of growth investing. This approach prefers to buy fast-growing companies and thinks that high price/earning ratios (P/E) are fine, so long as the company maintains higher-than-average growth and sales. The main point is to always buy the *best* companies, often regardless of price.

Benjamin Graham and his disciple Warren Buffet are the names most often identified with the Value Investing school. The idea here is to buy out-of-favor stocks. "Buy a company at a substantial discount from working capital, and sell it when it nears a value of 100 percent of working capital." Depending upon the market cycle there can be less risk to this approach, as the stock is already selling at a discount and with a lower than average P/E.

Here's a brief comparison of the Lynch and the Graham/ Buffet approaches:

GROWTH INVESTING	VALUE INVESTING
Peter Lynch	Warren Buffet
Most popular stocks	Out-of-favor stocks
Higher-than-average P/E	Lower-than-average P/E
Buy high, sell higher	Buy low, sell high
Planetary ruler: Jupiter	Planetary ruler: Saturn

You will notice that in the case of Peter Lynch, Jupiter is the planet most elevated, at the highest point. It is conjunct between the Midheaven and the Nodes. What does that mean? That he is a growth investor par excellence. Peter Lynch's approach to investing, "Buy what you know and like," shows up very clearly in his horoscope (see Fig. 3-1). Note the prominent configuration of Moon (Acquire) in aspect to his Sun (what you know) and Venus (what you like).

On Warren Buffet's birthday, the Sun is in close trine to Saturn (see Fig. 3.2). We also see that Mercury, the planet of stock-trading style, is involved with both Mars and Saturn. This shows his interest in value investing. Mars also may be strong, as it shows up in several contrarian strategies, one of which is Value Investing or buying out-of-favor stocks. Also, the fact that Mars–Saturn are together shows a strong retentive tendency. You will note that Buffet usually does not sell stocks as they approach 100 percent valuation, as called for by the "textbook" Graham value approach.

"To every thing there is a season, and a time to every purpose under heaven...." That famous line from the third chapter of Ecclesiastes, regarding timing, is often quoted by astrologers, and for good reason. Clearly, traders and investors go through "good" and "bad" periods. When they are on a hot streak it seems as if almost anything they touch turns to gold, and, conversely, when they feel like they are walking with a perpetual rain cloud over their heads, almost nothing seems to help. Astrology does help in timing these cycles, it being of particular value in both these cases to know when they will *end!*

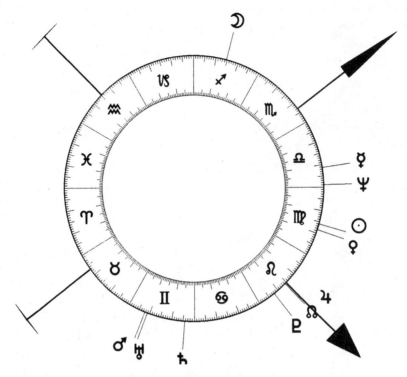

FIGURE 3-1   Peter Lynch's horoscope.

As the nature of the markets is always changing, we must be very wary of being the general always preparing to fight the last war. Market advisors generally are required to issue a disclaimer along the lines of "Past performance is no guarantee of future results." How interesting it would be if they were to post their upcoming horoscope indicators, in addition to past performance histories. This would allow for the fullest possible disclosure, I believe.

A surprising number of advisers and company presidents are becoming more and more forthcoming with their birth data. This is especially true of newer, small companies that will welcome any-sized investor. On the other side of the coin, some of the most successful futures traders like George Soros and Paul Tutor Jones, both of whom are rumored to use astrology, do not seem to have even their birth date readily

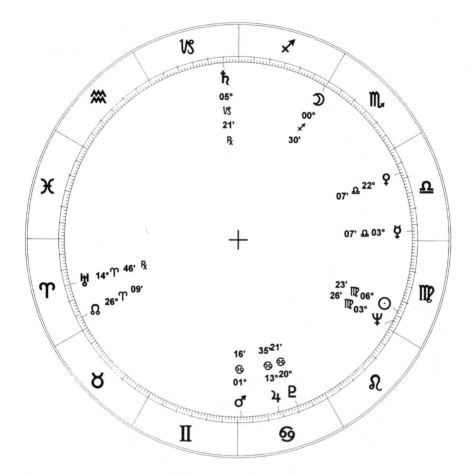

FIGURE 3-2 Warren Buffet's horoscope. Note that because Buffet's birth time is unknown to us, we have followed standard astrological practice in calculating a solar chart for sunrise, and have not included the Asc and MC.

accessible to the public record.* A very good idea, if you wish to keep your trading positions a secret!

Ignoring a client's astrological cycles, as many are wont to do, can lead to surprising results. While a few highly success-

---

*In a recent Soros biography the author, Robert Slater, wrote: "Whenever biographical details appear, whether in press releases put out by Soros-sponsored organizations or Soros's bios, the day and month of birth are omitted. Only the year is given. The reason is not clear." I disagree. I believe the reason is *very* clear. For example, on September 15, 1992, when Soros made a billion-dollar bet against the British pound, did it not show up in his horoscope? Wouldn't other hedge fund traders have wanted to benefit from this "insider" knowledge? Another small point: His business address is 777 7th Avenue, 17th Floor. A numerological coincidence? Maybe he's just naturally lucky....

ful financial astrologers disagree, I personally do not believe that one should *not* trade under the so-called bad aspects. How *should* one act under them? Cautiously! Traders should not only be more conservative but should *never* go against their system at these times. Discretionary traders should look for more confirmation and very strong signals before acting. This is true for systematic traders also. Both must keep very, very tight money management controls at these times, which of course aren't the best to gamble on a highly speculative investment of *any* sort.

Given a choice, it might be better at these times to lie on the beach than to be slaughtered by the markets. Still, one can't hide under the bed from one's horoscope. After all, the ceiling can still fall in on you! Caution certainly is well advised under a Saturn transit, and Neptune transits suggest that a strong reality check is in order. But these are just general guidelines, meant to give you a flavor of how financial astrology works. There are so many exceptions to these rules that I recommend you see your local astrologer in order to benefit from detailed, *personal* timing advice.

Sometimes the attempt to cheat one's fate can be almost comical in its effects. I recall vividly one trader who is especially mindful of ominous horoscope indications. Under a particularly poor aspect in which he felt that he would lose money, he decided to go against his own market instincts and bet against himself. He reasoned that at this particular juncture this approach was certain to make him a winner. Well, of course, his market instincts had been right. All he did by fighting against them was to create a self-fulfilling prophecy, and lose his money. Today, under similar astrological circumstances, he often simply takes minivacations, which he can well afford.

Let's now turn to an example of just one financial astrological factor, initially popularized in the postwar period by Mary Vohrzek, one of the unsung pioneers in the field. In her introduction to the McWirther classic *Astrology and Stock Market Forecasting* she writes:

There is one extremely important calculation to make, and this is the one for the "fatal flaw" point not only in your chart, but also in the chart of the stock or election chart. This point is called "the Mars/Neptune midpoint" and refers to that area in each where there is likely to be great disappointment because of miscalculation or unrealistic expectations as well as inherent susceptibility to error.... If this midpoint is aspected in your chart by current lunation or eclipses, it is a warning to you to exercise extreme caution in your affairs during the ensuing period. If this midpoint is activated in the foundation chart of some company stock you are considering, you should make a very careful analysis of current market activity and rent stock holder reports before risking your money.

My personal favorite example of the Mars–Neptune contact was its extreme prominence in the horoscope of the *former* republic of South Vietnam. Enough said...

I know that many of you would like to stop reading at this moment, and immediately call an astrologer to have the Mars–Neptune midpoint calculated. But please keep in mind that this is only one out of 78 midpoints that financial astrologers use in their calculations. According to Vohrzek one should also look at the Mars–Neptune *sum,* giving you still another 78 factors to consider!

In astrology, each trade itself can be charted. Every trade has a "birth"—the time, date, and place it was initiated—and a "death": the time, date, and place it was closed. Is it really possible to know whether a trade will be successful, just by knowing when it began? Yes and no.

Exercise: Make a list of your best and worst trades/investments. Note the date and, if possible, the time of day when the decision was made. Perhaps you will discern a simple pattern, such as that you tend to make money in the mornings or to trade poorly in the last week of option expirations. Perhaps you trade certain stock or industry groups well, but not others.

If you find this to be the case, you already know what to do. If no pattern is discernible, the next recommended step is to present your list to an astrologer. But in looking into this, either personally or through your astrologer, I believe you will discover a high degree of correlation between your most (least) successful trades and the cosmos. However, this mantic (prophetic) financial astrological approach is far from infallible, and some financial astrologers would consider it to border on the superstitious.

The Secrets of Horary Astrology

One very useful financial-astrological secret is to time the exact *moment* when your broker or anyone else offers you a market tip, or your trading partners ask for your advice on whether to do a given trade. The guidance you are seeking is often found by astrologers in the charts of such moments. Numerous rules pertain to the branch of astrology called *horary* (from *horos*: time), and we should take note of two of them here. First, if you are timing a question that has been asked, it must be a *real* question. One can't cheat the universe by asking a question idly, or if you don't like the first answer, asking it again and again. Second, you must always look at the chart of the inquirer *in relation* to the horary chart. This gives important information, not only as to the validity of the question itself but as to whether an appropriate answer has been generated.

Two Examples

Example #1.   I generally avoid penny stocks, which trade on the Bulletin Board or the Vancouver Stock Exchange. The primary reason is that they are generally less liquid and more limited in terms of disclosure than larger cap stocks. (Of course there are exceptions.) In addition, they provide a fine test of astrology. When one client called me to check up on a possible hot Canadian stock called Vidatron a few years back, for some reason I became personally interested. The story was acceptably good: The company was going to produce cost-saving medical videos for doctors. This was during the Clinton reign of terror on drug stocks. The horoscope of the call had Jupiter rising, generally an automatic *Yes!* signal in horary astrology. I therefore decided to buy 5000 shares at less than 50 cents a share, and it tripled within three months.

Example #2. My trading partner once called me to suggest that I sell silver future contracts. My own astrological and technical work suggested that the play was too early. I looked at the Astroclock on my desk and it showed a prominent Neptune. This represents a big question mark in horary astrology. That is to say, the answer is still a question, and not ready to be answered. So I declined. Silver rallied, and then later in the month fell, as we both had believed it would.

You may be thinking "we're getting awfully magical and hocus-pocus here." Next you'll be wondering whether I am going to suggest that you look into the entrails of sheep mark the flight migration paths of birds. "Couldn't I just as easily use a dartboard, or throw dice?" Perhaps. But astrology has been practiced for thousands of years, with *results*. Speaking from personal experience, I can only tell you that *it works*.

Again, as a possible exercise, write down the significant moments when such questions are asked. After compiling a list of times, you don't have to *do* anything. Simply note which would have resulted in successful trades or poor investments. Especially note those that were the most/least successful. Then present all of the timed questions, *without comment,* to a professional astrologer. I believe that many of you will be shocked by the results. Unless of course I'm talking to someone who already consults a trusted family astrologer on a regular basis. Telling *you* that astrology works is just bringing you old news.

Synastry (Syn = with; Astres = the stars)

Synastry or relationship charting covers:

1. People
2. Markets
3. Industries
4. Stocks

$$1 + 1 = 3$$

People.   Chemistry, or perhaps alchemy, makes life not only more interesting but, from a financial astrological point of view, more profitable. What I'm asking here is "Does your broker, financial astrologer, or trading partner complement you? Are your different weaknesses canceled out—or augmented?"

I have my Moon in Libra, which is an astrological-shorthand way of saying that I like to work with a partner. I find that when I'm focusing on the daily picture it's best for my partner to focus on the long-term picture, and vice versa. If he or she enters a trading position, it's often more profitable for me to choose the exit parameters, and vice versa. If he or she is good working with certain markets and technical patterns, it's usually best that I concentrate on other things.

One learns from bitter experience not to ignore *synastry*, the branch of astrology that deals with chart (people) comparison. In my earlier days, even with a relatively poor chart contact, I would too often override a poor chart comparison in the name of free will, or because I felt I had little to lose. Rarely, if ever, profitably. Those "great" deals offered at a questionable time, or by a questionable chart or chart contact have almost always ended up adding to the debit column.

Markets, Industries, and Stocks.   Over the years, traders slowly discover which markets they are most comfortable with. Initially, beginners imitate the trading style of their mentor or their favorite author. It takes time to find that one personal style, market, industry group, or individual with whom one is in tune. With strongly favorable horoscope indications, technical tools hardly seem necessary. Some people trade particular stocks with great success. We may specialize in covering certain industries, partially due to life circumstances. For example, I watch the computer industry quite closely, as I ran a computer company for many years. There is astrological verification for this. Of course if you only use computers and systematic trading, you may not agree. Unless of course you make a list of your greatest successes and failures and present them to an astrologer without commentary. Their matching up of the winners and losers may be a great eye-opener.

Market Timing
and the Art
of Prediction

Apparently, an absurdly obvious prediction. "I predict that at 3 P.M. a plane will leave New York's LaGuardia airport and head for Washington, D.C."

In fact, I could make the same prediction every day and be right over 90 percent of the time. I wouldn't achieve 100 percent accuracy, though, because on some days the weather would prevent the 3 P.M. shuttle from leaving on time and occasionally there would be a labor dispute or some other interference with the regular schedule.

Now the interesting point here is that much of astrological prediction works in very much the same way. We refer to a timetable, which instead of the OAG (Official Airline Guide) listing is a more universal guide, listing daily planetary positions, known as an *ephemeris*. We look up the "planetary schedule" for the day in question and make a forecast based on our subsequent study of events that have occurred when the planetary positions were in the same or similar positions and/or relationships in the past. This table should help you to understand.

Similar Astronomical Events

EVENT	DATE	MARKET ACTION
#1 Eclipse	January 15, 1991	100 point DJIA move (up)*
#2 Eclipse	November 3, 1994	100 point DJIA move (down)
#3 Eclipse pair	April 15–29, 1995	100 point DJIA move (up)

*This move can take place within a few days of the eclipse or between a pair of lunar and solar eclipses, which take place in a two-week period. As an example take the eclipse of October 24, 1995. Between October 23 and 25 the market moved down just two points. On October 25 and 26, however, the market moved down 80 points on a closing basis. The point here is that while the real trick is to note which way the move will go, strong volatility is relatively easy to forecast.

Gann and the Planets

By Greg Meadors

W. D. Gann, the legendary Wall Street trader, used many eso-teric techniques to predict future market directions and price targets with amazing accuracy. In the present context the word *esoteric* means "understood by only a chosen few" (Webster). These techniques were never revealed in any systematic way, and many of the principles that Gann drew upon in his fore-casting system still await your discovery. Some of them can be deduced from some of Gann's fictional writings, which on the surface don't appear to have much to do with the market.

One such book is *Tunnel Thru the Air,* in which Gann reveals some of the methods he employed to gain his success. The esotericism of Gann's forecasting is well known, but less so is the ancient body of esoteric sciences upon which he drew, including numerology, astronomical cycles, astrological interpretations, time cycles, Biblical symbology, sacred geome-try, and Gann's Law of Vibration. These methods comprise the keys to stock market timing. For example in *Tunnel Thru the Air* Gann advises reading the Bible to learn about cycles and about the manner in which the Creator reveals nature's uni-versal laws.

To acquire some knowledge as to the effects of cosmic influences you can read *Cosmic Patterns,* by J. H. Nelson. Nelson was an RCA scientist who discovered significant correlations between the angular harmonic relationship of the planets and those sun spots that affect short-wave-radio transmissions. This discovery made it possible for him to forecast future radio disturbances with a high degree of accuracy, based upon various planetary harmonic alignments.

For example, the widely hailed August 1987 Harmonic Convergence (see *Newsweek,* August 17, 1987) was a matter of several planets coming into conjunction (same longitude). This powerful congregation of planetary influences also formed a grand trine (multiple 120° harmonic alignment) with the outer planets, which culminated in the August 24th new moon at the top of the 1987 bull market, which in turn was followed by the October 1987 crash!

Another planetary cycle that occurred at this time involved the planets Jupiter and Saturn, which are considered cosmic opposites in astrological interpretation. Saturn is said to govern time and depression, while Jupiter is said to govern expansion. On August 19, 1987, Jupiter went retrograde (a condition in which a planet appears to be moving backward when viewed from Earth). This condition, said to decrease Jupiter's positive influence, lasted until December, a market low. At the same time Saturn turned in direct motion, which increased its depressive influence. Students of price activity should note that in 17 of the last 20 years the Dow Jones Average has tended to move sideways or lower during the 3½-month cycle in which Jupiter is retrograde. (See Fig. 4-1 for an example.)

Another natural-law effect involves the sensitive degrees of eclipses and the electromagnetic disturbances that often occur. On September 22, 1987, a solar eclipse occurred in the Earth sign Virgo, a portent of future market direction. On October 6, Mars (action) passed over this solar eclipse degree, activating a negative Mars eclipse energy. Venus also passed over the previous eclipse degree, and it was here that the market started its record-breaking 13-day drop. This was a text-

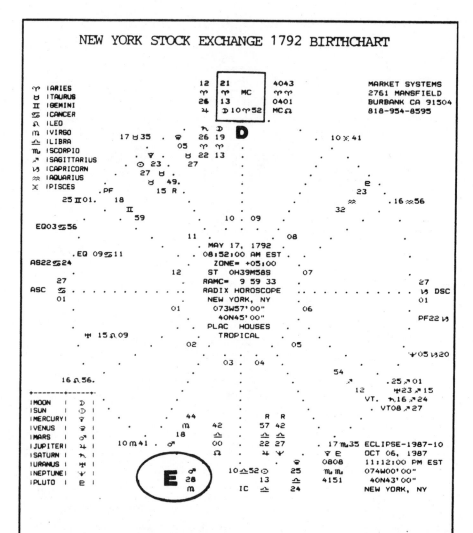

The *Encyclopedia of Astrology,* by Devore (1947) states: "Eclipses on the places of the Sun, Moon, Ascendant, or Midheaven (M.C.) are however, unfavorable influences. Frequently their effects are not felt until some time thereafter, when another planet, principally Mars, transits (passes) over the degree on which the eclipse occurred."

The Lunar Eclipse at the 13th degree on October 6, 1987 fell on the NYSE Midheaven (D). At the same time Mars (E) passed over (conjunction) the September 1987 Solar Eclipse Degree (29 Virgo) generating an extremely negative influence. (Isaiah 13:10)

FIGURE 4-1   New York Stock Exchange 1792 birth chart.

book astrological event [see the *Encyclopedia of Astrology* (1947), by Devore, on planets passing over eclipse points]. Mars then formed the negative square (90° aspect) with Neptune (confusion, delusion, illusion) exactly on October 16. In addition, Venus entered the bear sign Scorpio and formed a powerful conjunction with the destructive planet Pluto (Plutonium). The "bomb was dropped" when this conjunction was exact, on October 19, 1987!

During the October 1987 crash, Mercury (trading) was also conjunct Pluto at 8° Scorpio at the time of the 13° lunar eclipse on October 6. Around October 13, Mercury turned retrograde at 13°, in Scorpio, which presides over that eighth house of the horoscope which is said to govern other people's money, death, and destruction. Mercury also was harmonically aligned with the eclipse. The advanced student also should note the degree of the April 1987 lunar eclipse, the position of the fixed star Arcturus (the bear-watcher), and the other planetary alignments with this (bear-watcher eclipse degree) during the October 1987 crash.

The number 13 is a powerful number in ancient symbology. The Dow high was 2722 (2 + 7 + 7 + 2 = 13) in 1987, and this number vibration (with the planets) also provided an indication of a change in market direction. These and the other technical indicators gave advance warning of the tidal wave of selling pressure in October 1987, which came thirteen years after the October 1974 low.

Another stock market planetary cycle that has been of use in predicting short-term trend changes involves the standard 12 harmonic aspects between the planet Venus and Uranus. The most accurate is the trine aspect (a 120° geocentric angle). When other planetary indicators are not negative, the stock market tends to move up two or more weeks prior to the completion of the Venus trine Uranus aspect.

Gann also mentions the number 266 in *Tunnel Thru the Air*. The Galactic Center is located at 266° of longitude (26° Sagittarius). Examine any geocentric ephemeris and note that the market crashed on October 24, 1929 (Black Thursday), when the planet Saturn (depression) was at the Galactic Center (26° 22´ Sagittarius). Saturn has a 29-year cycle.

Would it not make sense to be prepared for a possible drop in the market when Saturn again reaches the same location in the heavens? Would it not also be of significance if this date were the second Saturnian anniversary of the 1929 crash, occurring on January 8, 1986? For the market *did* drop dramatically on January 8, 1988, when Saturn was again at the Galactic Center!

Planetary returns, cycles, and cosmic events that have correlated historically with previous major turning points provide information important to stock market timing. For example, the October 19, 1987 crash came exactly 50 years after the crash of October 19, 1937. When you have finished your research and discovered these historical relationships, you will then have the knowledge to forecast markets with a high degree of accuracy.■

It is in determining *exactly* when expected events will take place that the "craft" aspect of astrology comes into its own. While there are numerous rules in this area, they should be taken only as guidelines, not as precise formulas to copy. As a general rule one must look to any confluence of effects as the most likely time of manifestation. That is to say, we astrologers try to find a time(s) when several important influencing factors are present. The major factors in astrology are the slower-moving outer planets, Jupiter through Pluto. Astrological triggers are in general the faster inner planets, the Sun (Earth) and Moon, and the Ascendant and Midheaven (time and place of day). However, trigger events happen frequently.

Picking a Lock

Charles Jayne, one of the early pioneers of financial astrology in this century and a personal friend and teacher, taught that planetary timing is somewhat like picking an old-style lock. First you click off one cylinder, then you pick the next cylinder, and finally and only when the last has been released will the lock open. I never asked Charles on what life-experiences he had modeled this theory, but it makes an apt analogy regardless.

Cylinder 1:   Outer planets (Jupiter, Saturn, Uranus, Neptune, Pluto)

Cylinder 2:   Inner planets (Mercury, Venus, Mars)

Cylinder 3:   Sun

Cylinder 4:   Moon

Cylinder 5:   Ascendant and Midheaven

Unfortunately, the application of this theory is a little beyond the scope of this introductory work. It is meant to show that *several* astrological factors *must* be present in order to activate an event. In most of the examples that follow we will be demonstrating just one cylinder to make the relevant point. This leads to an important question: Since events happen all the time, how do we differentiate among them and find the *important* ones?

This is why we need to refer to the previously mentioned Rule #2 in our astrological forecasting: *Big events show up with big indicators.** The corollary also is true: *Big indicators show up with big events.*

As previously mentioned, when astrologers refer to big indicators they are talking about the involvement of the slower, outer planets (Jupiter to Pluto). These types of events happen more infrequently than trigger events. These outer-planet transits show up with the bigger stock market moves. The faster planets—Mercury, Venus, and Mars—when not backed up by the outer planets, correspond to the everyday trading activities of the market. Another *big* indicator of events are planetary clusters, and/or when multiple outer-planet configurations are involved.

---

*The astrologically savvy also will be familiar with the full axiom: The slower-moving a planet is, the more important it is in its effect; the faster-moving a planet is, the less important it is in its effect but conversely the more important it is as a timer.

SAMPLE INDICATORS	AVERAGE FREQUENCY	IMPORTANCE
Jupiter–Saturn square	Once every 10 years	Very
Nodal cycle ingress	Once every 2 years	Very
Solar eclipse	2–5 per year	Medium
Lunar eclipse	2–5 per year	Medium
Mercury retrograde	3 per year	Medium
Sun–Moon hard aspect	8 times a month	Low
True noon	Daily	Low

Here's a technical point that may seem very strange to the non-astrologically trained: *Every planet maintains its own integrity.*

PLANET	TIMING
Mars	Early
Neptune	Very early
Saturn	Late
Uranus	On time

Mars and Neptune aspects come early, Saturn aspects come late, Uranus aspects precisely on time. It is this type of astrological thinking that differentiates a classically trained astrologer such as myself from a purely "scientific," computer-based modeler. I typically draw upon this type of reasoning when making my specific market forecasts.

Some financial astrologers would maintain that one reason "expected" market declines often come later than "expected" is that astrological rulership of bear markets is under Saturn. Of course, the fact that financial astrologers also note the put/call ratios is another! If you are unfamiliar with this concept, consider one poplar market model, the gambling establishment. The odds are with the house. When everyone is betting the same way not only do the payoffs decrease, but curiously, that view is often wrong, i.e., the house loses money until the preponderant direction of betting changes.

The Cyclic Nature of Change

Much of life is predictable. The earliest astrologers noted rhythmic patterns in nature. Each day the Sun rose and set. Each month the Moon waxed from new to full, then waned to new again. Every year there were seasonal cycles from spring to summer to fall to winter and back again to spring. Over the course of time numerous longer-term planetary cycles were noted and compiled. At some point these cycles were correlated with events on Earth. Not only was there metaphysical truth in nature—birth-development-death-rebirth—but somehow in the dawn of man's history these cycles in nature became part of astrological practice. Astrology was thus both an awareness of man's place in the cosmos and a tool for conscious participation in it.

A commonly noted seasonal pattern is the tendency of the U.S. stock market to fall during the fall. September and October often are "down months." The financial panics of 1929 and 1987 both occurred in October. Other notable "fall" times were 1873, 1947, and 1974. In recent years the major stock market declines all have occurred in October, in the years 1989, 1990, 1992, and 1994. (See Fig. 4-2 for more information on the crash of October 1987.) Given the increasing tendency of the market to self-reinforce discovered cyclic patterns, they are very likely to continue.

"This Time It's Different," or Cycles and Investing

Financial astrology can be a telescope and/or a microscope. In other words, financial astrologers chart both cycles and unique cosmic/terrestrial events, intermediate- and long-range trends, as well as forecast short-term and intraday market moves.

Jupiter and Saturn are known as "the business planets." The 12-year Jupiter cycle and 27-year Saturn cycle play a role in the economy. There are many more such astronomical cycles, such as the 19-year nodal cycle. We astrologers also keep our eye on an important 60-year cycle, based on Chinese

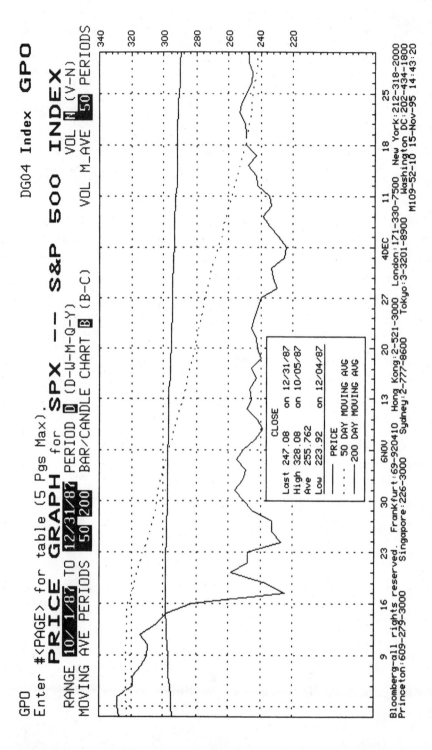

FIGURE 4-2 October 1987 month graph. (*Courtesy of Bloomberg.*)

astrology. Each 12-year period (Jupiter cycle) is associated in turn with each of the five elements of Chinese astrology: Fire, Earth, Metal, Water, and Wood.

Not surprisingly, according to cyclic theory it is *never* different *this* time. Yes, there are both evolutionary and disruptive changes in the markets. But whether in 1929 or 1987, eventually market valuation approaches some semblance of reality.

Long Cycles and the Master Time Factor

By Richard Mogey

Two of the early researchers in long cycles were N. D. Kondratieff and W. D. Gann. Kondratieff described a cycle of between 48 and 60 years. (See Fig. 4-3, which shows the 60-year cycle plotted below yearly corporate AAA bond prices.) This cycle, known as "the Long Wave" or "the Kondratieff [K] Wave," has become one of the premier cycles in market cycle research. It also has become one of the most interpreted and popularized of all cycles, with every author seeming to make greater and wilder claims about its effects than another, with facts playing as small a role as is possible. Good research has been done on this cycle, although as is generally the case, it hasn't found its way into the popular press. The "K-Wave" is not what many think, but it is an important cycle.

Another author who has referred to a cycle of similar length is W. D. Gann. His work and the commentary on it make the popularizers of Kondratieff look like the most rigorous scientists who have ever published. Apparently Gann himself was deliberately enigmatic, as were those who carried on his tradition. As far as can be demonstrated to unbiased researchers, Gann never stated absolutely just what his Master Time Factor is, although apparently he referred to it as

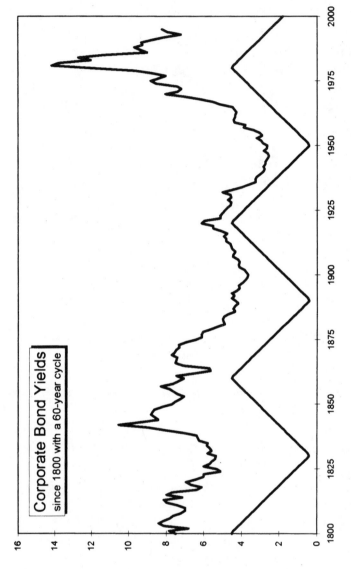

FIGURE 4-3 Mogey graph.

being three cycles of the Jupiter–Saturn cycle of 19.589 years. This is the time it takes for Jupiter and Saturn to form a conjunction. Every three cycles they make a conjunction in the same part of the sky. Many have considered this to be a totally irrelevant bit of planetary lore. After all, what could Jupiter and Saturn have to do with markets or the economy? The answer is "more than many ever thought," and more and more evidence in support of that statement is coming in all the time.

The Evidence

Prior to the advent of satellites, few scientists had any confidence in the idea that anything extraterrestrial could have any effect upon human or animal life. Yet since the first satellite went into orbit, data has continued to pile up in support of a planetary-solar-terrestrial connection. First it became clear that solar changes are dependent upon the large outer planets, primarily Jupiter and Saturn. The Sun is not the center of the mass of the solar system but is pushed and pulled by the large outer planets about the true center of mass known as the *barycenter*. This pushing and pulling can be measured through the conjunction of the two largest bodies, Jupiter and Saturn. When they are conjunct they are both on the same side of the Sun, pulling the Sun farther from the center of mass. When they are on opposite sides of the Sun the center of mass tends to be near the center of the Sun, depending upon the alignment of the other important planets. What is remarkable about these planetary-solar changes is that they have a significant effect on the climate of the Earth. These climatic changes in turn affect commodity prices. Commodity prices drive interest rates, and interest rates drive the stock market and the economy.

If this was the whole story, it would be interesting enough, but there is an even more significant correlation. Virtually every significant cycle in stocks, commodities, and interest rates is either a multiple or a harmonic of the Jupiter–Saturn cycle. The Greeks called this cycle "the Great Marker of

Time." For example the most important long cycles in commodities and in interest rates are the (59.577 = 3.19.859), the 178(178.731 = 9*19.859) and the 536(536.193 = 27*19.859). What is curious about these cycles is that each is three times the other.

Equally remarkable is the division of this cycle in stocks. Stocks that are driven by interest rates don't show long cycles because they can respond positively and negatively to both sides of a long interest-rate cycle. The most dominant cycle in stocks is the decennial pattern or 10-year cycle (9.9295 = 19.859/2). The next important cycle is the 40-month cycle (39.718 = 19.859/6). Of lesser importance are the 5-year (59.577 = 19.859/4), 4-year (47.662 = 19.859/5), and 2-year (23.831 = 19.859/10). This cycle also marks the 78-, 39-, and 20-week cycles within just a few tenths of a month. There are no single numbers that dominate in the way that 3 does in multiplication. All of these cycle lengths have been deduced by Fourier analysis as well as induced by visual inspection. They are universally considered to be the most important cycles. They also make sense from an astronomical point of view.

In addition to these cycles there is an even more curious relationship between two of the most dominant short cycles, the 73.762 and the 16.135. Fourier analysis continually reveals both of these at work in the stock market, and they are exact divisions to three digits of this cycle (19.859/70 = 73.762 and 19.859/320 = 16.135). These of course are less significant, especially since the divisions get finer, although it is very curious that the lengths are exact.

Clearly the work of Gann involved some knowledge of the planets, and the evidence shows that he successfully used the Jupiter–Saturn cycle as a master timer. (Whether this was his so-called Master Time Factor is open to debate.) Kondratieff was an economist used to studying data, and his work pointed to this important cycle. Had he had more information on the effect of the planets on solar activity and of solar activity on the Earth's climate he might have been better able to understand the long wave.

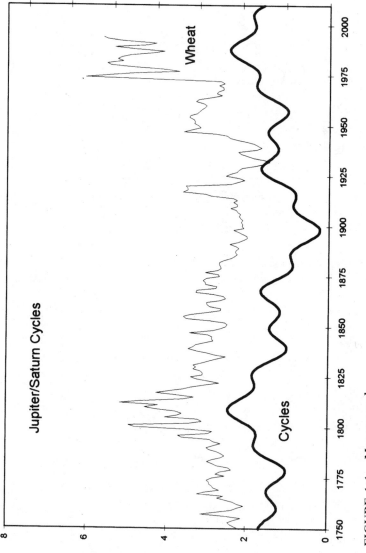

FIGURE 4-4. Mogey graph.

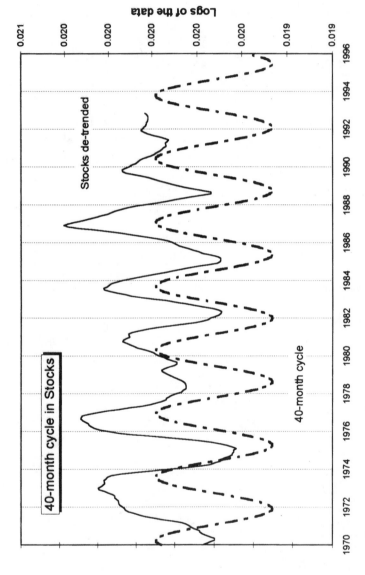

FIGURE 4-5   Mogey graph.

It must be added that all cycles work together as an organic whole, and therefore this cycle, no matter how important, simply plays one role in the whole drama and does not determine every change either in prices or in interest rates. (See Figs. 4-3, 4-4, and 4-5.)■

Shorter-term Rhythms and Trading

Mark Liebowitz, author of *The Volume Reversal*, tells of how he first met astrologer Norman Winski on the floor of the Chicago Mercantile exchange. The stock market was up 15 points. Norm pointed to the clock and said that the market would reverse in *exactly* 10 minutes. Within three seconds of the designated moment the market started down, to close at a then-unusual eight-point loss on the day. From that point on, Mark began to take note of astrological cycles.

The most-watched cycle is the lunation cycle, or the Moon's monthly change from new to full that takes approximately 28 days. Full Moons are well noted not only by bar owners, who regularly see a marked increase in business, but also by traders, who regularly find increased market volatility. If I had a dime for every occasion on which a trader has said to me "The Markets are wild [or crazy] within a day of the Full Moon!" I would have sufficient money to buy a small yacht.

In general, astrology breaks up the lunation cycle into four weekly sections: New Moon, Quarter Moon, Full Moon, and Third Quarter. The New Moon is the beginning of the cycle and is generally considered a good time to enter into a new position. The first and third quarters are test or crisis points, while the Full Moon not only exaggerates expected market moves but often can be accompanied by a short-term change of trend. This corresponds to a period of change from increasing light with the first half of the Moon to decreasing light in the second half of the lunar month. Some traders simply add the time of the New Moon and Full Moon to their technical charting methods as potential turning points, especially when correlated with similar technical indicators.

A well-known astrological saying goes: "What the New Moon promises, the Full Moon delivers." Financial astrologers often break up the monthly cycles into New-to-Full, and Full-to-New components. Two especially noteworthy lunations are the Solar and Lunar eclipses, which correspond to certain new and full Moons. These can correspond to *dramatic* changes. An example here is the January 15, 1991, solar eclipse, corresponding to the Gulf War, and the subsequent 114-point market rally the next day.

There are many intermediate-term cycles in astrology. Among the most popular are the retrograde cycles of the planets, at which time they appear to be moving backward. This is a purely geocentric effect, as the planets never actually move backward. Think of riding a local train when an express train passes you. You *appear* to be moving backward in relation to the train that is moving faster than you. The most critical times are when the planets move from Direct to Retrograde (also called "Stationary RX") and from Retrograde to Direct (also called "Stationary RD"). Each such period can be considered to be one unit of an intermediate market movement. Frequently there is also a short-term market reversal at one of these times.* Ignore these periods, if you wish. Personally, after losing almost $30,000 on one such period, I have vowed *not* to ignore them in the future.

A similar story was told to me by Greg Meadors, one of the acknowledged rising stars in financial astrology.

> Yes, I have one, my own story about how I lost a small fortune in three months in trading options [before discovering Gann/Astrology indicators]. What a dummy I was! Completely new to the market, and I thought I knew what I was doing. It started in 1985. I was aggressively long in September on call options when *Jupiter went retrograde* in July 1985. Naturally they all expired worthless in September,

---

*See Appendix II for a list of New Moons and Full Moons, and for RX periods of the planets in 1996–2001.

just before the *big* rally. Had I bought in September instead of early July, I would have made half a million in three months.

But then, if I didn't get thrown off that horse, I might not have looked into astrology for the markets. When I found correlative evidence, I couldn't believe it. I set out to disprove it. However, the deeper I looked, the more "gems" I found.

From Chinese calendar astrology we have four important and very useful time divisions consisting of daily, day, monthly, and yearly cycles. There are many more such cycles worthy of investigation. To gain further information on the subject I would suggest that the interested reader contact the Foundation for the Study of Cycles, which is the leading research organization on cycles.

High/Low Market Charts

Another technique astrologers have in their grab bag is to compute a chart for the exact time a market has made the last significant high or low. Just as *place* holds importance in technical analysis, so too *this time/place* has significance for some financial astrologers. While I generally don't chart this myself (one must make choices in the number of techniques one uses), such a chart can sometimes provide one with interesting information.

For example, if they had looked at the high of the Tokyo chart of December 29, 1989, astrologers would have noted two important configurations. First, a Moon–Saturn–Neptune conjunction that translates to: Moon (publicity) for a Saturn (rock) on a cloud (Neptune). We also have a Sun–Uranus–Jupiter opposition, which many financial astrologers would instantly recognize as a possible overextended condition of excessive optimism.

The big question after the Tokyo market crash was "When will it recover?" Let's look to some astrological clues. Our goal is to see the true bottom within the "false" one. Our procedure is to calculate a horoscope chart for each of five instances, then compare it to the market-top horoscope.

The astrological definition of False (Neptune) Bottom (Saturn) is the Saturn–Neptune midpoint. There is of course a plethora of information in these charts that can be gleaned by astrology, but here I wish to stress principles and guidelines only, three of them being these:

False bottom #1	Saturn–Neptune = 19 Capricorn = Moon in Top Chart.
False bottom #2	Saturn–Neptune = 15 Capricorn = Saturn in Top Chart.
False bottom #3	Saturn–Neptune = 0 Aquarius.

In an August 20, 1995, article in *The New York Times* on the Japanese market, Ken Brown writes: "And the Nikkei has touched four false bottoms, in April 1990, September 1990, August 1992, and November 1993. Rather than soaring from those spots, each time the market rose just a few thousand points only to fall again." The article questioned whether the most recent low of June 20, 1995, at 14,485 was the beginning of a turnaround.

Please note the following 6 pivotal points:

All time high	December 29, 1989	38,916
False bottom	April 13, 1990	29,214
False bottom	Sept. 28, 1990	20,983
False bottom	August 14, 1992	14,820
False bottom	Nov. 26, 1993	16,726
False bottom?	June 30, 1995	14,485

This point is not as significant in the top horoscope, and could therefore be a potential bottom. Astrologers would also note the Sun–Pluto Square present, which could also indicate a possible reversal. This occurs in time just below a natural major technical support level of 15,000. We thought this might hold, but why buy? At the time we saw no compelling reason to buy into Japan. Subsequently the Japanese market went nowhere for three years, except for yen appreciation. We recommended Japanese Bonds as a much better buy at that time for yen principal appreciation, although our advice fell on deaf ears.

False bottom #4   Saturn–Neptune = 6 Aquarius = Venus in Top.
False bottom #5?   Saturn–Neptune = 24 Aquarius 40 = MC in Top.

At first glance this point equals the MC, and so we might conclude that it is another false bottom. However, what is most interesting is the *exact reversal* of the Midheavens between this and the 1989 market top. Therefore, this *may* hold, although a third retest of 15,000 is quite possible. (See Fig. 4-6 for a false bottom graph.) Given the fundamentals of Japanese banking, there is some chance the market could fall to a final support level of just above 12,000. In any case we still expect to see 22,000+ in 1997, and thus we recommended a possible first entry. Appropriate hedges for yen also were suggested (shorting 120–125, unhedged around par, or 100).

Remember, in global markets the most money is made by keeping currency valuation in mind. For example, those who played the long side of the U.S. market in the first half of 1995 made more money by also shorting the U.S. dollar at the same time. We believe the most money will be made after 1996 by selling the yen above 120 and buying the Nikkei below 15,000.

Like the race car driver who turns to the camera before performing a high-risk stunt for TV, we caution our readers that this strategy definitely is *not* for everyone, for if you are wrong you will be *doubly* penalized. Currency trading is difficult even with the help of financial astrology. Markets have a way of defying gravity and/or reality for *very* long periods of time, so *be careful.*

By the way, if you're checking for False (Neptune) Tops (Jupiter), look to the Jupiter–Neptune configuration.

When I first began studying the stock market I was often given a simple explanation for a market move, such as "Today

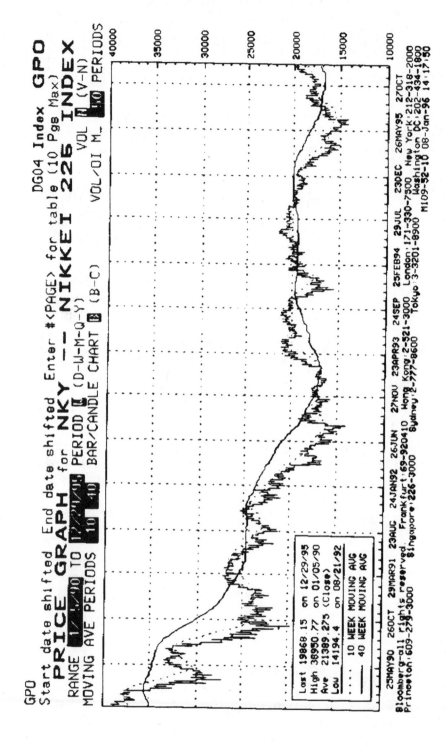

FIGURE 4-6 A graph depicting false bottoms. (*Courtesy of Bloomberg.*)

the market was up because the bonds were up," while the next week "the market was down and the bonds were up [in a flight to quality]." Later there came more elaborate explanations: "Traders took the news as an excuse to take profits." Like most of the facile explanations offered us on the TV news, these explanations were by and large only a convenient face-saving gesture for analysts.

Profit-taking probably *was* a good "reason" that day, but why *that* particular day, at *that* particular price level? One might just as well say that the market was up because the market wanted to go up. In fact *that is the answer*, and one that makes perfect sense from an astrological point of view. Just like individuals, the various markets and their components of stocks, futures, etc., have horoscopes. These horoscopes show "good" and "bad" days just as people's do.

One knotty problem is misinformation. What for example should be done with a report that was "inaccurate" (i.e., the next month's revised report proved to be substantially different)? Financial astrologers often will point to Neptune as the culprit. That is, reports issued under the influence of Neptune seem to have a great tendency to be in error or at least highly unclear. Another example is when the bond market "incorrectly" calls for an interest-rate cut by the Fed that does not occur. But isn't the market, as the sum of all available information, "always right"? This recalls the old philosophical problem: "If a tree falls in the forest and no one is there to hear it, does it make a sound?" Of course, if you know the answer to that one, or to the Zen koan "What is the sound of one hand clapping?," you probably have no need of astrology to help you trade the markets!

Anyway, eventually I decided to choose a theoretical line as representing "reality" or "full evaluation," with the market periodically agreeing with or intersecting this correct or full valuation line. Most readers would argue the reverse: that periodically my model catches up to "reality," i.e., the market. Nonetheless, all agree that it is most profitable to trade the *extreme* of a trading market, shorting extreme overvaluations and buying undervaluation. Note however that this strategy can fail miserably when one is wrong about the markets, i.e., if it is in a trending rather than a trading mode. More on this later.

Initially, my astrological training suggested that it was most important to forecast *events*. Eventually I realized that it's more important, or at least far more profitable, to forecast *markets*, and to worry less about which excuse is given by the media. So we may be expecting a crisis in Mexico or South Africa but instead it occurs in South Korea, a country I usually don't cover. That sits fine with me, so long as I get the right market reaction.

As an example, one Sunday evening we were On Watch for expected major trouble in Japan. It turned out that the originating cause was Singapore, and the Barings Bank crisis. No matter. Our trader, who usually doesn't cover that market, stayed up late (past 11 P.M. New York time), and was fully prepared and quite happy with the profitable trading results obtained. Do remember that trading in commodities and derivatives, unlike stocks, is a zero-sum game. The fact that Barings Bank lost hundreds of million of dollars means that others *made* hundreds of millions of dollars because of the crisis. Did they use astrology? Given the striking clarity of the case, and the popularity of astrology in the Far East, I believe it is a fair assumption that at least some of the winning traders did.

One of our landmark forecasts was the Gulf War, first predicted the day after Bush was inaugurated in 1989 on the basis of his inauguration time. Astrologers chart the exact moment a president takes his oath of office as one primary indicator for his administration. More than two years in advance we forecast a U.S. military conflict for mid-January of 1991, eventually refined to being only *four hours* off! (Not being military astrologers, we did not include adjusting the time of the strike launch to allow for pitch black aerial combat concealment in our forecast.) However, on that particular bet we *lost* money, even though previously we had made two killings because of it (January 9, our greatest oil call, and also in late December). I remember well everyone laughing as we called for a 1200-SP (limit) drop on January 9. By noon I was being taunted by some traders, who were kidding me about my extreme forecast. They laughed until about an hour and a half later in the early afternoon when it actually occurred!

Yet the majority of people who believed the war would not take place were long, and vice versa. I have already given the example of one financial astrologer who predicted a California earthquake yet lost money by shorting insurance stocks. It could be well argued that he should have studied the horoscopes of the insurance stocks as well. But that isn't the point I wish to make here. I am now recommending that you concentrate on the market reactions themselves and *not* on what *appears* to cause them. My early career is loaded with correctly timed "negative news stories" that the market stubbornly shrugged off and chose to ignore.

Playing Volatility

Early in my career I was surprised to learn that to certain traders, this is more important than market direction: "Henry, if you can tell us how much the market will move, that's all we need. If you have the direction too that's nice, but not necessary." This is because they made most of their money selling option volatility. These periods are best revealed by monitoring a sequence of rapidly alternating cosmic patterns and by noting any subperiod that is sharply defined within a countertrend of a major cycle. The five primary indicators of volatility that most financial astrologers look at are these:

1. The lunation and eclipse cycles
2. The sunspot cycle
3. Planetary groupings of contrasting planets
4. The alternating influence of contrasting planetary pairs (e.g., Jupiter and Saturn)
5. The planet Uranus

Because astrology charts not only cycles but also unique

events, this does help one to make money in the market. The story of two famous forecasts, of the U.S. and Japanese stock market crashes, follows. The first, as I have already mentioned, had much to do with moving me from being a GP (general practitioner) astrologer to a financial astrologer. The second was the forecast that was destined to establish my reputation as a financial astrologer of some repute.

Forecasting
the Crash of 1987

By Charles Harvey, D.F. Astrol. S.

It has often been reported that Michael Harding and I "forecast the 1987 crash to the day." This is true and yet also misleading, for it gives a distorted picture of the kind of projections astrology can make and the kinds of inferences an astrologer can reasonably make from a study of astrological cycles. For whilst astrology often can be remarkably accurate at identifying the overall direction and trend and the precise turning points in markets, it is, unaided by other techniques, usually much less precise about the likely magnitude of any particular move, and may sometimes identify a single turning point that marks a high in one market and a low in another. The unvarnished story of what we forecast almost a year earlier for October 1987 is shown in Fig. 4-7, which is an exact reproduction of the relevant page of a market letter that we prepared for the specialist company Chartsearch in November 1986.

This figure originally was part of a Chartsearch financial newsletter, issued to its clients in December of 1986. As can be seen, we projected that the London market as measured by the FTSE 100 index (which usually but not always runs closely parallel to the New York S&P) would rise strongly during

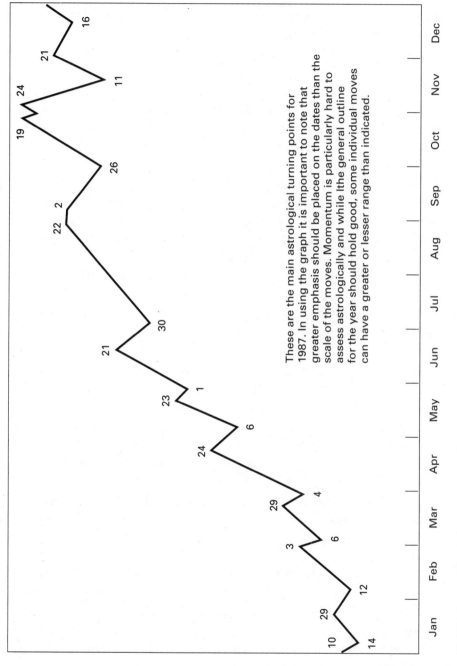

These are the main astrological turning points for
1987. In using the graph it is important to note that
greater emphasis should be placed on the dates than the
scale of the moves. Momentum is particularly hard to
assess astrologically and while lthe general outline
for the year should hold good, some individual moves
can have a greater or lesser range than indicated.

FIGURE 4-7 FTSE 100 projection for 1987.

the year into August and October, peak out October 19–24, then make its steepest fall of the year to November 11 before recovering. At that point we saw the market running on up to end the year higher. In fact the markets in London and New York made secondary peaks early in October, and of course ended the year more or less at the levels at which they had begun.

A comparison between our projection and what actually happened in London and New York shows that we were essentially correct about the main trend of the market and various key turning points, and that our time designation of what we saw to be the major fall of the year was almost exact. It started in earnest with the massive plunge down on October 19, and bottomed out on November 10. We did not foresee the magnitude of the fall, and did not specify in 1986 that this major correction would take on "crash" proportions. Furthermore, we envisaged the market running up into October 19–24, whilst in reality it ran out of steam around October 2–5. Yet in practical terms the chart offered a valuable guide to what was going on. In fact, as the market began its final run-up through September, I was able, in the light of my knowledge, to alert clients to the fact that in view of the overextended state of the market it would be prudent to expect a "very major correction" around October 19–24 and crucial to be out of the market by mid-October. Likewise, on November 11, I was able to advise clients with a reasonable degree of confidence that it was probably now safe to get back into the market, the worst being over.

I will explain in a moment the main astrological basis for our reasoning on the 1987 market, but first I think it's important to point out that in the late autumn of 1986, when we were preparing our 1986 forecasts, markets both in the United Kingdom and the United States were considered to be already relatively overextended and at a plateau, and probably heading for a correction. The general consensus amongst non-astrological financial analysts at that time was that 1987 would be unlikely to show much improvement over 1986. Thus in projecting a dominantly bullish year with a strong uptrend into the autumn, we were already sticking our necks out.

The other factor you should keep in mind here is that whilst the major planetary cycles that seem to regulate overall optimism and pessimism as well as specific levels of confidence and anxiety for investors and business decision makers are common to the world as a whole, each stock market does have its own idiosyncratic way of responding to these cycles. Likewise each country has its own politico-economic agenda and mechanisms (such as interest rates and currency policies) that have their impact on the extent to which a given market will follow particular planetary cycles. In this respect New York and London, as relatively "free markets," tend over the years to run in close synchrony.

Let's turn now to the rationale behind the projection Michael Harding and I made for Chartsearch in the autumn of 1986. This was the result of several years of intense computer study and analysis of the New York and London stock and precious metal markets. The Chartsearch projection was an attempt to synthesize our understanding of how the various different phases and interactions of the planetary cycles that we and pioneers like W. D. Gann, David Williams, Clifford Matlock, and others had identified would be likely to express themselves in the market.

The three dominant cycles that seem to determine the rise and fall of the market in general are those of Jupiter, Saturn, and Uranus (though the Saturn–Pluto cycle, as I have shown elsewhere, certainly plays its part as well). Jupiter relates to expansion, opportunity, and optimism. It is the Greed factor in the market; Saturn by comparison is the hard-nosed, "nitty-gritty," value-for-money, and ultimately Fear factor in the market; Uranus by contrast is the Promethean, "fire-stealing" principle, which relates it especially to new technologies and innovations. Combining these three cycles, and studying the way they are triggered by the energizing, entrepreneurial energy of Mars, can open one up to a good bit of the major market trends of any given period.

Technically the slowest of these cycles is the 45.35-year Saturn–Uranus cycle, which seems to mark out the main pulse of the ebb and flow of "applied technology." Indeed, a case can be made for the assertion that the geocentric conjunction of these planets on May 3, 1942, as world industry geared up for total war, marked the beginning of the major, technology-fueled industrial cycle that has driven the market ever since. In 1987 this cycle was nearing its close, with the next conjunction due on February 13, 1988, which point, like May 3, 1942, would be a theoretical low point for this cycle. Taken by itself, this cycle pointed to a significant low in early 1988.

Yet the Saturn–Uranus cycle appears to work together within the overall constraints of a triple, 59.58-year Jupiter–Saturn cycle, which makes what W. D. Gann punningly called his "Master Time Cycle" (after the fact that Jove is significator of Kings and Masters, and Saturn is the Roman name for Chronos, the God of Time). This cycle seems to mark out the dance of optimism and pessimism, of greed and fear, of investment confidence and lack of confidence. This roughly 60 year cycle is usually measured from its peak period of enterprise, in the years which occur around the time when Jupiter and Saturn are in conjunction in Capricorn (as in the years around 1901 and 1961), and from the troughs, when Jupiter is in its strongest sign (Cancer) opposing Saturn in its strongest sign (Capricorn), as in the periods around 1930 and 1990.

Within this 60-year cycle, Jupiter–Saturn's single cycle of almost exactly 20 years (an average of 19.86) pulses out a sub-rhythm of expansion and contraction.

This 20-year cycle is, coincidentally, synchronized with the decades, so that Jupiter and Saturn tend to be conjunct in the first year of one decade and in opposition in the first year of the next. Because of this pattern, the same-number years in each decade often tend to have a similar flavor and market pattern. This is most consistently the case with the fifth year of each decade, which is usually close to the Jupiter square Saturn when, true to form, as we saw in 1995 and as we predicted in May 1994, the market normally rises over 30 percent. In this cycle the seventh year is less consistent but often shows a strong fall in the autumn (as in 1917, 1937, 1957, and 1967). Yet in 1987 the critical autumn phase was preceded by a sustained period when Jupiter, in the most enterprising and enthusiastic of the Fire signs, Aries, was applying to the normally buoyant and optimistic trine of Saturn in Sagittarius. We viewed this as boosting the market throughout much of the year, not only because it was itself a very classic "boom" pattern but because Jupiter was simultaneously forming a long-term trine to Uranus, so that Jupiter–Saturn and Uranus were all exceptionally powerfully linked over an unusually sustained period.

The Jupiter–Uranus cycle of approximately 13.81 years is one that has long been associated with optimism, innovation, technological breakthroughs, and a Promethean sense of omnipotence. In the stock market, especially approaching the trine phase, it normally is marked by considerable confidence, buoyancy, speculation, and "partying." During 1987 Jupiter, from February 12 when it left the square to Uranus in already enthusiastic Aries, was moving toward the first exact trine Uranus on June 21 and then stayed within orbs right through its station on August 19 until it again trined Uranus on October 24. It was obvious that once this aspect was exact, "the party was over." This view was reinforced by the fact that following the close of jollifications, Jupiter was then due to run backward toward the opposition of Mars on November 11, which so often in such contexts marks a key burnout bottom in the market. Of course we then considered that as Jupiter moved to the trine of Saturn in November and stationed in December, then started to move again to the trine of Saturn and Uranus in February, the party would pick up again. It gradually did, but from a vastly more severe setback than we had anticipated in 1986.

So why did we think that October 19 would be a key date, and the start of a major setback? We had two reasons. The first I am not at liberty to reveal, but I can tell you that, invisible to most astrologers, the Master Time Cycle was at this point in one important respect *in an identical phase to its position on the day of the 1929 crash.* The second reason was that on the 19th the Sun, which is so often the final trigger for the manifestation of a planetary pattern, came into the opposition of Jupiter and the trine of Uranus, completing the "circuit" of this energy pattern. This is a classic trigger pattern normally required to release a slower cycle, and it suggested very vividly that the 19th would be the day on which it would become clear that the party was indeed over. Wrongly, we conjectured that the remaining days of the Jupiter–Uranus trine would bounce the market back up before a final loss of enthusiasm on the 24th. In fact those final days of joviality showed Jove at his most enthusiastically destructive, expanding the panic and volatility and wreaking havoc on those who had had the hubris to imagine that "the market is different this time."

In concluding I would suggest that the above-mentioned cycles, together with some others including Pluto, Mars, and the annual and the lunation/eclipse cycle, sound out a hidden music which in large measure calls the tune the markets must dance to. At present some financial astrologers can sometimes pick out the main tunes with remarkable precision, sometimes with far less certainty. In due course, and after further sensitive listening to the celestial symphony and its harmonic structures, the waltzing, jiving, tangoing, and rock-and-rolling of the market should become relatively predictable. Presumably at that point the market will enter a period of self-conscious crises, not knowing how to cope with so great a threat to her essential mystery. But for quite a while yet, she is certain to keep us guessing.■

Predicting
the 1987 Market Crash

By Arch Crawford

When I first heard about using astrology to predict the stock market, I was a technical market analyst for Merrill Lynch.

Back in 1961–1964 I was the first-ever assistant to Robert Farrell, who has for the last many years been considered the best technician on Wall Street. At that time I was spending most nights until midnight in the M.L. library, calculating 10-day moving averages on Advances–Declines, New Highs–New Lows, and just about every other figure that was generally available in *Barron's* or *The Wall Street Journal*. Then one day in April of 1963 an article came out on the front page of *The Wall Street Journal* about a man who had been predicting the market using astrology, and doing very well at it!

The story was about David Williams, for 40 years head of the purchasing department of the Consolidated Edison Company of New York. It was David who ordered the first commercial nuclear power plant from Westinghouse for Con Ed. He became interested in using astrology to predict the price of copper and thus obtain optimal buy points for his employer. He was also a lieutenant commander in the U.S. Navy during World War II. He had written a pamphlet called *Astroeconomics* back in the mid-1950s, which he expanded in the 1980s into a major book, *Financial Astrology*. As I was young and impressionable, and open to anything and everything that might help me in predicting markets, I ran out to a New Age bookstore and bought his pamphlet. On the same shelf was another, entitled *Stock Market Prediction* (1947) by Donald Bradley, so I picked that one up too, and of course a book listing the planetary positions (ephemeris) since 1890 or so.

Checking over the planetary alignments and comparing them with the Dow Averages, I was amazed to find a very noticeable connection. Even from just a cursory examination it was clear that large movements in the markets were coincident with particularly large groupings of harmonic "aspects" of the major outer planets!

The Bradley book contained a method of compiling a model projection for the market, taking into account *all* of the planetary aspects through a weighting formula. It was based on many assumptions of classical astrological meanings, plus observation by some of the better modern researchers. Surprisingly, the stock market would *often* follow this "sidereal potential projection line." Then for several months at a time it would go astray, only to come back to the projection somewhere down the road. I wondered what it would do if, instead of assigning a theoretical value to each aspect, we could compute and enter into this formula an accurate historical value for what had actually happened in the past, i.e., the average percent change in the Dow Jones every time this astrological occurrence had been repeated since the first recording of the Dow Industrial Average.

I kept the Bradley original-formula Projection Line for many years, and in 1974 I began to compute a number of the "actual" cycles. It took about a week to compute each one, using large accounting sheets and small writing. Adding together several of these self-generated cycles led to a very accurate projection. Yet there still were times when the market went its own way and ignored all projections, planetary or otherwise. One of those aberrations appeared when the Cycle Sum peaked in April of 1979 and started a long plunge into the projected *low* of November 7, 1979. The market continued to work its way higher, consolidated sidewise, then worked higher once more throughout the entire summer.

Frustrated, I sought to understand the planetary patterns that were developing. Looking ahead to the September sky, I noticed a massive, multiple-aspect configuration involving the five outermost planets, spread like the fingers of a giant hand at 30° intervals. That means that each was semi-sextile (30°) to the next one; that the first and third, second and fourth, and third and fifth were sextile (60° apart); that the first and fourth and second and fifth were square (90°); and that the first and fifth were trine (120° apart). Every one of these aspects became exact between September 2 and 23. The very day of the *last* of these connections the market made its *top*, then proceeded to dive into what became known as the Second October Massacre (1978 and 1979), making its low *exactly as on the predicted date of November 7!*

This is a prime example of how a unique planetary alignment can interfere with the smooth functioning of my Cycle Sum, or of Bradley's sidereal potential line.

The next time we came upon such a powerful exception was the Harmonic Convergence of the Mayan Calendar, August 24, 1987, and we were ready for this one!

In 1987 my Astronomic Cycles Sum line peaked in April, then began to drop off fairly badly during the summer and fall. Once more, as in 1979, the stock market continued to work higher and higher, with little or nor planetary aspect corroboration. This time we looked ahead and saw a dramatic sight: the Harmonic Convergence! Mr. Jose Arguilles wrote about this time, and the changes predicted for this point by the Mayan Calendar. He had somehow come up with the date of August 17 as the most significant to the astronomers of that former great civilization. An article about his work appeared on the front page of *The Wall Street Journal* a month or so before the event.

There didn't seem to be any special qualities to the day chosen for the celebration. Yet seven days later, on August 24, there was to be a conjunction, with five visible bodies (including the Sun and Moon) in 2¼° of arc, perhaps the tightest such arc for at least the past 800 years. It was clear to me that the Mayans were pointing to *this* spectacular event. With the similar type of experience of 1979 under my belt, I boldly wrote in my August 8 newsletter (titled *Harmonic Convergence*): "Our long-term sell signal is set in stone. Be out of all stocks by August 24, after which we will have a horrendous crash." *The Wall Street Journal* dated August quoted *Crawford Perspectives* as looking for a "decline" in the autumn, but the more flamboyant *OTC Stock Journal* of August 24 printed this front-page headline: ARCH CRAWFORD SEES LONG-TERM BEAR MARKET. The final line of that article read: "His recommended investments, for the time being, are treasury bills, gold, and put options."

The Dow Jones Average made its final lunge upward (to 2732) to 12 noon of August 25, only hours after the last of the multiple conjunctions. From there it worked its way steadily lower until September 8, rallied for about a week, then sank to new low ground on the morning of September 23, a most unusual day marked by a solar eclipse on the fall equinox.

After scaring away many traders that morning, the market reversed violently and closed *up* a *record* 70 points! It rallied for two weeks; near the rally peak, the largest earthquake in over seven years hit Southern California, centered in Whittier. The market was able to stabilize for two to three days before resuming its slide with a *record* drop of 96 points on the day of the lunar eclipse (October 6). From there it never looked back. The October 10 *Crawford Perspectives* was titled "NO SIGN OF A BOTTOM," but suggested possible turning dates of around October 21–22.

Friday, October 16, was a triple options-expiration date, and those who had written (sold) option contracts were desperately trying to lessen the damage to their positions by supporting the market until those contracts were finalized (on Saturday, at Friday's closing prices). The Dow had dipped to a loss of 135 points during the day, and this powerful segment was able to stem the tide to only a 108-point decline. On Financial News Network (the precursor of CNBC) we said on Friday, "In this atmosphere, we would not be surprised to see a 150-point down day, followed by a 200-point down day." That was the most negative statement we remember hearing from all the analysts who spoke up during this fateful period, but as it turned out it was not nearly negative enough! Options people sold on Monday all that they had accumulated on Friday, and much more. The Dow Industrial Average slumped an all-time-historic-record 508 points in a single session.

The next morning, Tuesday, the slaughter began anew. As more DJIA stocks began to open trading, it appeared that the market would be down another 200 points or so by 10 A.M. Before that hour, news (or rumor) was circulating on the exchanges that the Federal Reserve was making credit lines available to brokerages and to exchange specialists, and by 10 the Dow actually was in the plus column. There were huge swings over the next few days and it was two more weeks before the markets stabilized and based, making a reaction low on December 4, 1987. Some indices made lower lows in early December and many did not, setting up a Technical Divergence that proved the bullish (positive) case.

Although the Mercury station and Sun opposing Jupiter over the weekend prior to the crash may have exacerbated the emotion at the low, we believe that the determining factors were to be found in the astronomic pattern at the *top* rather than that at the bottom. Alan Abelson, editor of *Barron's Financial Weekly,* wrote of the crash in his column of October 26:

> Well, these analysts said it was because of…this and those analysts said it was because of…that. These Economists said it was…this and those Economists blamed…that. We'll just have to chalk it up to an *unharmonic convergence.*∎

The Japanese Stock Market Crash

By Henry Weingarten

To begin with, I wanted to establish my reputation by predicting the Tokyo Market crash. Clearly everyone *knew* it was coming, only no one knew exactly *when.* Many traders were losing their shirts shorting. As I would for a personal client, I drew up a three-year forecast for the Japanese stock market. Using horoscopes of the TSE (Tokyo Stock Exchange) and the Japanese nation made this a relatively easy forecast. (See Figs. 4-8, 4-9, and 4-10.)

Let's start by talking about why most traders were wrong. First, the fundamentals. There was *no* way the TSE was going to crash in the same way as the U.S. market did. The ruling LDP or Liberal Democratic Party was too much in control of the situation. The LDP monolith had to crack first, which it subsequently did. Now with the Saturn–Neptune conjunction (rock on a cloud) conjunction in 1989, life was getting more interesting for the TSE bears. The U.S. real estate market still was suffering from the aftereffects of the 1987 crash. Earlier,

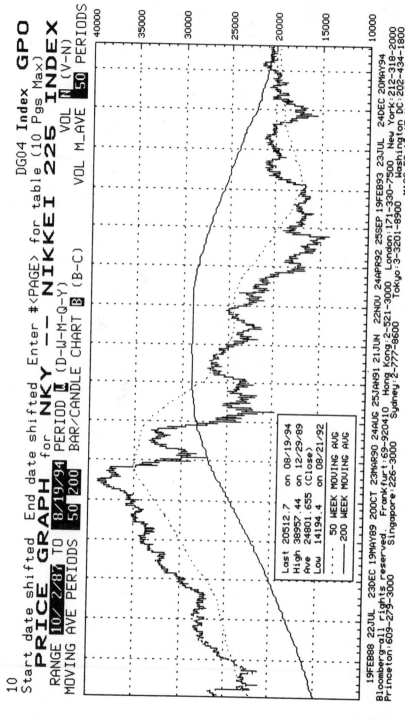

FIGURE 4-8 Tokyo Stock Market crash. (*Courtesty of Bloomberg.*)

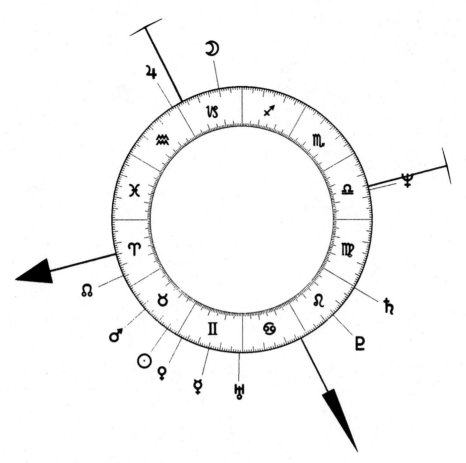

FIGURE 4-9   Tokyo stock exchange horoscope.

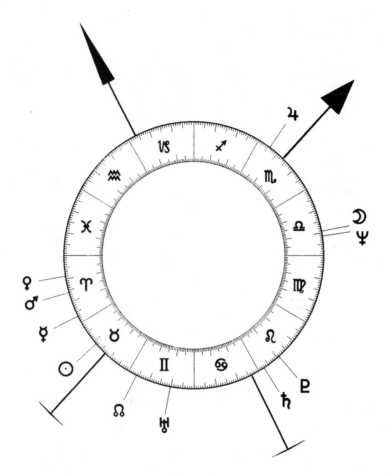

FIGURE 4-10   Horoscope of Japan.

the real estate boom's mantra had been: "Buy, buy, buy! Prices can *only* go up!" But in Tokyo real estate prices were so astronomical that even a small magazine store would sell for more than a million dollars! Something had to give.

Now let's try to reason as a good astrologer would have back in January 1988. "Everything is crazy, a major real estate crash is inevitable, and many, many players in Japan are going to be hurt *really* badly." What is the main indicator we want to find? Saturn. Yes, Saturn should be present for a fall, but Saturn can represent reality as well. (Saturn also can be a *pos-*

itive force in markets.) Let's see when Saturn is strongly affecting both the TSE and the Japanese national charts. We noted the conjunction of Saturn on the Ascendant in the Japanese national chart, and on the descendant in the TSE chart for March 1990."

Thus came our first possible indicator for the type of event we were anticipating. Of course I had to check many other factors astrologically, but this was the starting point.■

Selecting Markets

In general, I prefer the *top-down* approach to stock-picking. That is, I first make a general assessment of the overall market, *then* choose the more favorable industry groups, and *finally* select stocks within these groups that correspond well to the overall planetary themes.

Here's an example:

STOCK'S MOVEMENT	CORRELATION
Overall market conditions	50% +
Industry group membership	25% +
Individual stock pick	25% +

I agree with those market studies that attribute at least 50 percent of a stock's movement to overall market conditions, 25 percent to the industry group, and 25 percent to the individual stock itself. Of course there are times when we use the bottom-up approach, concentrating primarily upon special situations occurring for certain stocks (this will be discussed in Chapter 7), but try to understand the advantage of top-down. If we are incorrect about the unique desirability of a particular stock but right on the market and industry group, we still can benefit from 75 percent (50+25) of its move. If on the other hand we were to decide to buy a stock just before a major market correction, less would be gained. This argument often is made by market timers, of whom financial astrologers are among the biggest fans. Others claim it is impossible to reliably and consistently time markets. Naturally, I strongly disagree. Market timing is a lot like the oft-debated question of Fate versus Freewill: Even if we really *can't,* we mostly act on the assumption that we *can.*

Walking up the Down Escalator

Try to keep this idea in mind when you are stockpicking and ignoring a down secular market trend: Stock prices of even the best companies in the best sectors will *generally* do somewhat poorly in a strong down market.

For example, no matter how fundamentally solid that stock was that you researched in Mexico in 1995, it had little chance of going up. Why? Because the Mexican market was in a state of panic and you got hit with a double whammy at the collapse of the peso. (See Figs. 5-1 and 5-2.) However, we are following Mexican TV with great interest, as it will benefit from the upcoming planetary theme of entertainment with the Jupiter–Neptune conjunction of 1997. For the same reason, we are watching Brazil's Globo and other similar stocks.

One of our clear-as-a-bell warnings on the NAFTA debate came from the national horoscope of Mexico. I sometimes like to imagine the outcome of the debate between Ross Perot and Vice President Gore, if Perot had displayed as one of his charts the horoscope of Mexico, with the upcoming transits of Pluto/Sun/Mars in 1995. An astrologer would translate this planetary configuration as "potential crises, transformational changes, and possible violence." Would Gore still have won the debate? Who knows, but the journalists sure would have had a field day with that one. If it *had* happened, financial astrology would have been validated by the upcoming events in Mexico, and become an important part of future political debate. I know most of my readers think I'm dreaming here, but many revolutions have started with just such a dream.

Invest in Mexico in 1995? Just as the 1987 crash was a watershed even for financial astrologers, so too the Mexico crisis opened the eyes of even more Wall Streeters to the potential of astrology. The stock market crash of 1987, or the

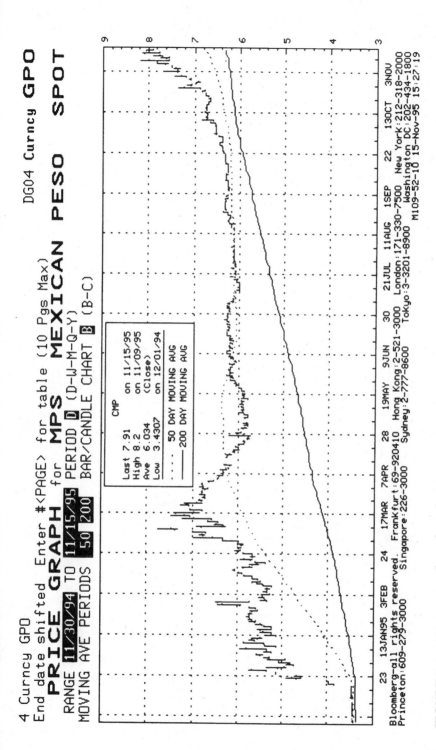

FIGURE 5-1 1995 peso technical graph. (*Courtesty of Bloomberg.*)

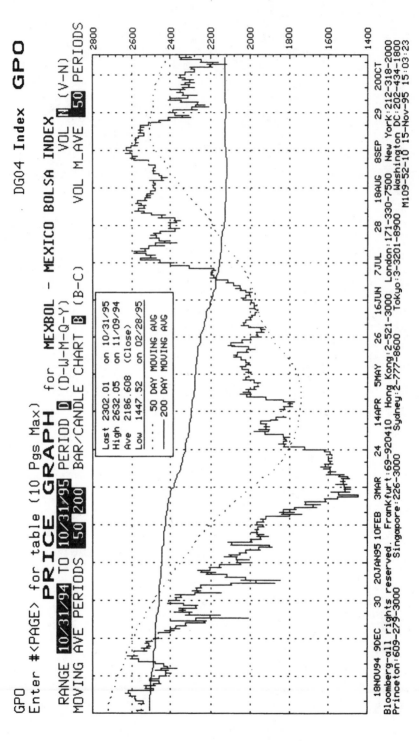

FIGURE 5-2 1995 bolsa technical graph. (*Courtesy of Bloomberg.*)

Tokyo market crash, were by and large not unexpected events to value investors. All that was in doubt was the timing and, in the former case, the severity and quickness of the crash. The Mexican crisis, on the other hand, took many more investors by surprise due to the highly propagandistic pro-NAFTA campaign that falsely said all was rosy with the Mexican economy. This misinformation didn't fool financial astrologers for a minute. Of course, the warning signs were clear to many savvy investors even without the benefit of horoscope analysis. Yet amazingly, as I write this in August of 1995, most seem oblivious to the upcoming second Mexico crisis. After selling at any cost earlier in the year, investors once again are buying Mexico.

We at the Astrologers Fund took the first crisis to be a *brief* buying opportunity, especially in other parts of the South American market. Yet we quickly recommended taking early profits. The risk of a second Mexican crisis was simply too great over the summer and fall of 1995, beginning with Pluto–Mars again activating Mexico's Sun. A fear of anarchy and the possibility that the country is on the brink of political and economic disintegration gives this investment a very poor risk-reward ratio. Why should investor confidence return when Mexican stability is so threatened, at least in the short term?

From a conventional investing viewpoint, Mexico had a poor risk-reward ratio, in comparison with the rest of South America. If the Mexican economy did well, the fundamentals were stronger in the rest of Latin America. If the Mexican market collapsed again, the rest of Latin America would fall less far and hard. In addition Telemex, which is often the surrogate for Mexico for foreign investors, had serious problems. Profits were poor, and in less than two years Mexico was scheduled to liberalize its telecommunication industry. Telemex could prove to be a very weak competitor. As for the peso itself, I often joked in late 1994 and early 1995 that while the dollar would soon weaken against "real currencies," it would remain preferable to the Russian ruble and Mexican peso, at least for the foreseeable future!

Having decided in the autumn of 1992 that we were quite
bullish on gold, we looked to make a number of recommendations. Literally almost any gold stock looked good to us, as
gold bullion was selling at $340, which seemed very cheap to
us indeed. We added the recommendation of overweighing
Australia. Our gold stock universe consisted of the United
States, Canada, Australia, and South Africa. We very much
liked Australia because the currency was far undervalued in
our opinion. Not only fundamentally but also technically and
astrologically, our trading signals were in major alignment. At
$.65 to the U.S. dollar, we expected a better than 7 percent
currency appreciation that year. That meant that if we were
right, and even if gold stocks were flat, we would increase the
value of our holdings 7 percent.

In late 1994 and 1995 we again liked the gold sector, because of an expectedly great weakening of the U.S. dollar versus other major currencies. The Mexican bailout disaster only
led us to strengthen these convictions. This time our preferred
country was Canada, a resource-rich country. We saw the
political problems as being minimal, specifically the Quebec
separatist threat, and we forecast at least a 5 percent currency
appreciation. Our "North America mantra" for 1995 was: "Buy
Canada, sell Mexico!" So we went hunting for Canadian gold
stocks and frequently recommended selling Telemex, the popular bellwether of the Mexican bolsa. (See Figs. 5-3 and 5-4.)

While currency work involves quite a number of factors
that we have omitted here, one of the most important is of
course the overall health of the country, a prime indicator
being a country's birth horoscope. (Examples are given in Fig.
5-5.)

Family Horoscopes

In choosing which markets to invest in, you have a cornucopia
of choices to draw upon. When helping you to choose a country we look at its founding horoscope, the chart of its prime
minister/president, the chart of its stock market(s) or the currency, and so forth. We can find further corroboration in the

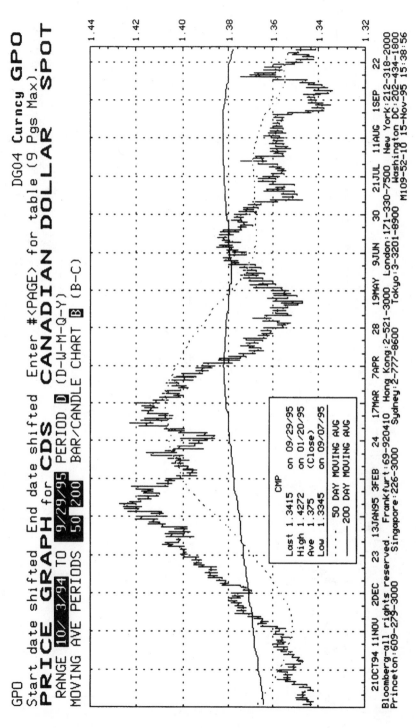

FIGURE 5-3   CD$ technical chart, 1995. (*Courtesy of Bloomberg.*)

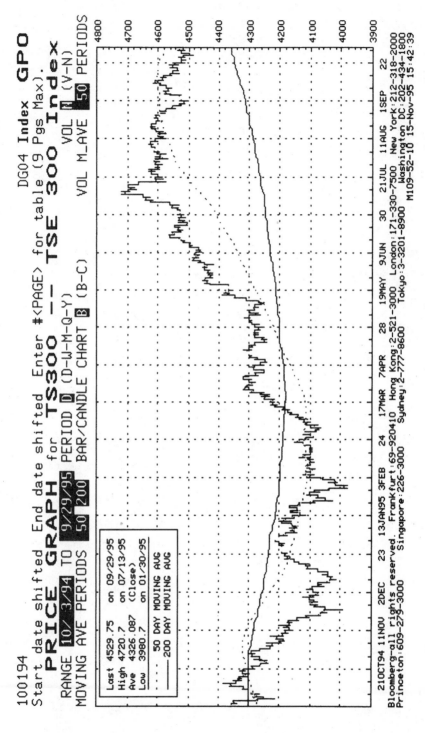

FIGURE 5-4 Toronto Stock Exchange 300 index. *(Courtesy of Bloomberg.)*

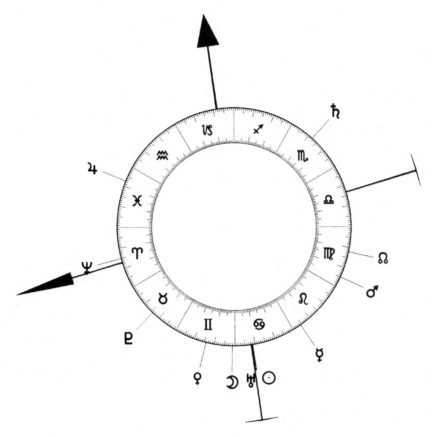

FIGURE 5-5   Horoscope chart of Canada.

charts of country funds. For example if more than one Mexican country fund shows potential trouble in early 1995, that is most likely telling us something. In the following three cases, Pluto, Uranus, and Neptune were prominent during the first Mexican market crash, while Neptune and Pluto hovered about through the end of 1995 and early 1996:

Mexican Fund (MXF):	1/13/81 Baltimore, MD
Mexican Equity and Income (MXE):	5/24/90 Baltimore, MD
Emerging Mexico (MEF):	6/25/90 Baltimore, MD

This principle of "family" horoscopes is extremely helpful

here. Imagine for a moment that an event occurs such as the death of one's wife. First of all, it should show up in your wife's horoscope. But as a major event it will also appear in your chart, the chart of your children, and the horoscopes of her mother and father. This shared event would show up in each affected horoscope. In financial astrology we have many choices. One can simply use one horoscope, such as the market horoscope, or several horoscopes, for better confirmation of significant market moves.

Unlike the successful buy-and-hold stock market strategy widely seen over the past twenty-five years in many developed countries, underdeveloped country markets can represent ticking time bombs. I certainly can't imagine investing in *any* emerging market without checking at least one and preferably several horoscope charts. The risk otherwise is simply too great for my personal tastes. If you are unfamiliar with them, these include a unique set of risks such as currency fluctuations, limited liquidity, less revealing financial reporting requirements, and "unpredictable" political developments. In a period of change, one expects to receive above-average returns. Investors who restrict their activities to the United States do not have these worries. This is why an increasing number of money managers do so, or else contract out this function to financial astrologers. Clearly the easiest situation to forecast is when there is an expected event such as an important political election. Other times it's more difficult, especially when confusing political/economic signals are prominent—the horoscopes sometimes simply reflect this confusion, rather than easily and simply resolve it.

Inflation

Furthermore, depending upon one's view of impending inflation, there is the relative mix conventionally made between bonds, stocks, and cash, which in my view should be extended to be bonds, stocks, cash, commodities, and real estate. Normally one looks to the thirty-year bond market for the built-in market view of forthcoming longer-term inflation.

Using the family horoscope model, we also look to receive confirmations from the gold and silver markets, and from the CRB indexes for intermediate-term views. Some smart money traders also follow the central bank horoscope charts closely, along with FOMC meeting data for short- to intermediate-term moves. This subject is quite complex and beyond the scope of this work. We mention it here simply for the sake of completeness and to guide the more experienced reader to fruitful fields.

The Four Types of Market Views

Here they are:

1. Confusing view—Confusing view
2. No view—No view
3. Mixed view—Mixed view
4. Clear view—Clear view

A final point: Not all markets are so clearly defined. There are many confusing time periods when the astrological signals are mixed and confusing as well. At other times there may be no major astrological signals. This lack of cosmic direction often corresponds to a meandering or sluggish market with, not surprisingly, "nothing happening." Mixed astrological signals correspond to a sideways market, but with more sharply defined alternating short-term trends. However, there are also many times when they are quite clear despite apparent confusion.

Upon their first exposure to financial astrology, many find it surprising that its technical signals act like other technical or charting systems. Why shouldn't they? Financial astrology is *not* magic, although to the uninitiated its practice may sometimes seem like it. Further, techniques among financial astrologers vary greatly, which is fine so long as they give consistently repeated and reliable results. One can use many different techniques as well as different charts, even borrowing heavily from the technicians' grab bag.

Selecting Industry Groups

A Brief Overview of Planetary Themes, 1971 to 2011

I attribute between 25 and 30 percent of a stock's price movement to industry-group membership. This is why I like to use
planetary themes to help me anticipate winning and losing market choices. While one can back-test financial market concepts
for hundreds and in some cases thousands of years, I like to
concentrate on the period from 1971 on—the start of the modern period of the New York Stock Exchange. (While founded on
May 17, 1792, it was reincorporated on February 18, 1971.)

Interestingly, there is a Moon–Jupiter–Neptune conjunction which I believe helped to pave the way for the increased
speculative/gambling casino quality of 1980s and 1990s markets. I grant that this may be a somewhat arbitrary choice.
Others would endorse April 26, 1973, as the establishment
date of the CBOE (Chicago Board Options Exchange), with
its subsequent launch of the SPX futures contract that forever
changed the once comparatively leisurely pace of NYSE. Dow
watchers can also point to November 14, 1972, the day when
the DJIA reached 1000 for the first time. In any case, we
know from family horoscope theory that we can discover similar multiple confirmations from a family of horoscopes.

Often there are three passes to these major outer-planet
conjunctions. The first naturally corresponds to the beginning,
but not until the last pass has occurred is the influence "complete." Further, we can allow for orbs of up to 1° to 2°, i.e., one
to two years in advance or after. Remember, the market doesn't
turn on a dime, and not only is an influence felt in advance
(after all, the market is supposed to be a leading indicator of
economic activity), but also its effect lingers. It's a little like a
fad making the cover of *Time* magazine. It certainly does not
represent the beginning of interest, and it will continue on
after that point, but the fad is probably near its maximum
impact at *around* that time. Here are three easy examples:

> Saturn–Neptune: March 3, 1989; June 24, 1989;
> November 13, 1989. Real estate bubble burst: Fall of
> Communism (Berlin Wall)

Uranus–Neptune: February 2, 1993; August 20, 1993; October 24, 1993 Anything goes.

Jupiter–Pluto: December 2, 1994 Mega-mergers; whales eating whales.

Looking to the upcoming major conjunctions of 1997, we see

Jupiter–Neptune: January 9, 1997

Jupiter–Uranus: February 16, 1997

Here are some of the recent times these conjunctions have occurred:

Jupiter–Uranus: December 11, 1968; March 11, 1969; July 20, 1969

Jupiter–Neptune: February 1, 1971; May 22, 1971; September 16, 1971

Jupiter–Uranus: February 18, 1983; May 14, 1983; September 25, 1983

Jupiter–Neptune: January 19, 1984

And forthcoming, again:

Jupiter–Neptune: May 27, 2009; July 10, 2009; December 21, 2009

Jupiter–Uranus: June 8, 2010; September 19, 2010; January 4, 2011

The Jupiter–Saturn cycle was nicely described by Richard Mogey on pages 75–81. Comparing the last cycle period of 1980–1981, we project the next one for 2000. Remember the eighties real estate boom? We believe this upcoming period after 1997 will be another good time to invest in real estate or REIT (Real Estate Investment Trusts).

Jupiter–Saturn: December 31, 1980; March 4, 1981; July 24, 1981

Jupiter–Saturn: May 28, 2000

For the sake of completeness we also provide you with the following time periods:

Jupiter–Pluto: November 2, 1981

Jupiter–Pluto: December 11, 2007

Saturn–Pluto: November 8, 1982

Saturn–Uranus: February 13, 1988; June 26, 1988; October 18, 1988

Industry Groups

This discussion is not intended to be complete. We start at the conjunction or beginning of the cycle of each pair of outer-planet cycle groupings. Let's take the planet Jupiter's cycles as one illustrative example:

Jupiter–Saturn	Real-estate, construction
Jupiter–Uranus	High technology
Jupiter–Neptune	Entertainment, pharmaceuticals
Jupiter–Pluto	Oil, biotechs, banking

Outer-planet transit aspects in astrology have the most weight, i.e., are long-term and important. These cycles can be subdivided in a number of ways. One primary division is by 4: the 90, 180, and 270 aspects. We also can consider the entire hard-aspect series (multiples of 22 ½), and can find significance in even so-called minor aspect series of multiples of 7 ½ or 11 ¼. For example, when Saturn was 270° Pluto on 3/20/93, 10/09/93, and 1/2/94, almost every day the newspapers were full of stories about one company after another laying off personnel. Because it became so prevalent, downsizing was renamed "rightsizing" in order to help justify unprecedented defensive belt-tightening, even by corporations that were highly profitable. After the influence of the aspect passed, some layoffs continued, albeit no longer in a feverish, first-page-news fashion.

Political and Planetary Fortunes

Astrology can offer us some insight into changing political fortunes, insight that may have important market consequences. For example, foreknowledge of the Clinton presidential victory in 1992 was a great trading signal to short pharmaceutical stocks.* It was also crystal-clear at the time that a great reversal of political fortunes would take place in 1994. This facilitated the relatively easy forecast of a longer-term drug-stock rally, especially when taking into consideration the forthcoming Jupiter–Neptune conjunction of 1997, which also favors this industry group.

Clearly, foreknowledge of political events has enormous market consequences. This is why there is a full branch of financial astrology, called *mundane astrology*, that covers world events and geopolitical trends. There are many techniques and heuristic tricks used to predict U.S. elections. Of course astrologers look first at the charts of the presidential candidates. They also study whether similar success aspects are to be found in the charts of the vice-presidential candidates. We look at daily charts on the first Tuesday in November and on inauguration day in January.† Some astrologically savvy presidents, such as former President Reagan, slightly adjusted the time of the swearing-in ceremony to jibe with the rules of electional astrology. Further confirmations are possible through a check of synastry: chart comparison of the presidential nominees to the horoscope of the United States, monthly lunation charts in January for the "feeling" tone at that time, and so forth. A large number of techniques may be used.

---

*Unfortunately, due to use of bad data, this was not my forecast, spoiling a previous seven out of seven correctly predicted presidential races. This error is discussed in some detail in Appendix II. The second part of the forecast, regarding drug stocks and the 1994 midterm elections, *was* a success.

†Because a number of the founding fathers were masons and astrologers, originally the election day in November was trine (in favorable aspect) to the March inauguration day. Both were trine to the birth horoscope of the United States. This Grand Trine was considered to be highly favorable. Unfortunately, it was changed during the Roosevelt administration and there was no longer any consideration given to the astrological consequences of making this election cycle shift.

Selecting Stocks

Selecting stocks by looking at the incorporation time* corresponds to fundamental analysis. The incorporation is the birth of the company, and as with human beings, tells us of its basic strengths and weaknesses. It also is the key reference point for predicting its future. Interesting studies by index funds claim that as many as 79 percent of professionally managed stock funds *underperform* the S&P 500 Index. Astrologers like to believe that they not only can time markets but are good stock pickers. But can the fund managers who employ financial astrology really do both?

Financial astrologers first check to see if the signature is valid, e.g., whether Uranus, the planet of technology, is strong in a technology stock. If this planet is not strong, they highly question its future in the technology sector. For new issues this can be extremely important, as the company may not have what it takes to succeed in its business field. Similarly, financial astrology provides one with an interesting view of the consequences of merger and acquisition activity. Financial astrologers analyze the potential benefit of the fit by referring to the horoscopes of the acquiring and acquired companies. There are rules for good synergy and whether it's a good time to acquire the company. Being naturally cautious, I always prefer to buy prospective M&A candidates with strong horoscope fundamentals, as this promises long-term profits regardless of whether a proposed takeover succeeds or not.

There are advantages to studying the horoscopes of the 30 DJIA stocks, as they also give clues to general market direction. Unfortunately, for this very reason they do not always give the clearest, most precise indications. This is because these stocks often are bought and sold to meet overall market option plays. However, a strong individual indication almost always wins out. So even in a case like IBM in 1994, where the market viewed the stock negatively, we could confidential-

---

*Astrologers will immediately see close, strong contacts. For example, the incorporation chart of IBM has Sun with Uranus, Dec Moon with Uranus, HWP Sun with Uranus, Apple Sun with Uranus, Intl Sun with Uranus, etc. In Appendix IV we list sources for the incorporation and first listing times of thousands of the most important U.S. stocks.

ly predict that it would reach or exceed the price of 100 by May 1995 based on the strong Jupiter configuration to its birth horoscope at this time.

Astrologers please note: When analyzing non-OEX 100 and SP 500 stocks, you will not run into this interference from program trading.

Astrology as a Telescope

As a former owner of a computer company, I still watch the industry closely. Digital Equipment Corporation is a personal favorite of mine, and not only because of its extremely high beta (volatility). Let's look briefly at DEC at its all-time high in 1987 (Fig. 5-6) as well as its all-time low in 1994. The former was an ideal time to sell, and the latter a good short-term buy.

Please note these key astrological factors as seen in Figs. 5-7 and 5-8.

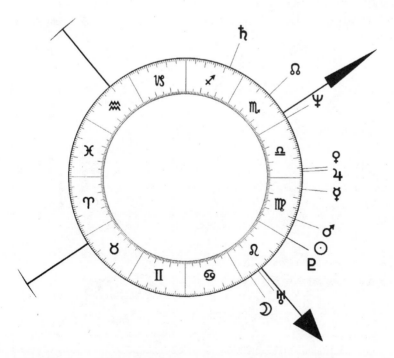

FIGURE 5-6   DEC natal chart.

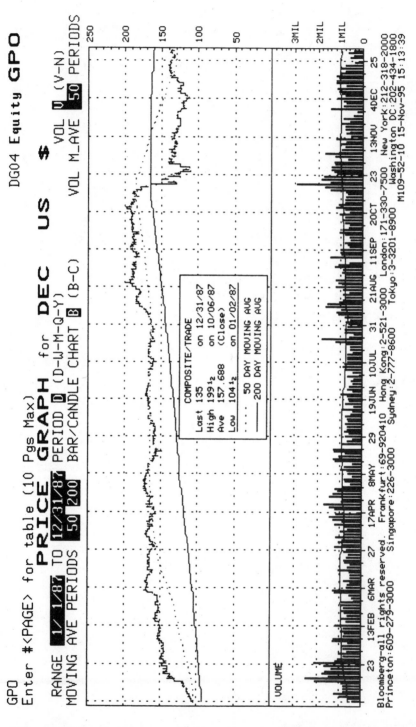

FIGURE 5-7   DEC high chart (1987). *(Courtesy of Bloomberg.)*

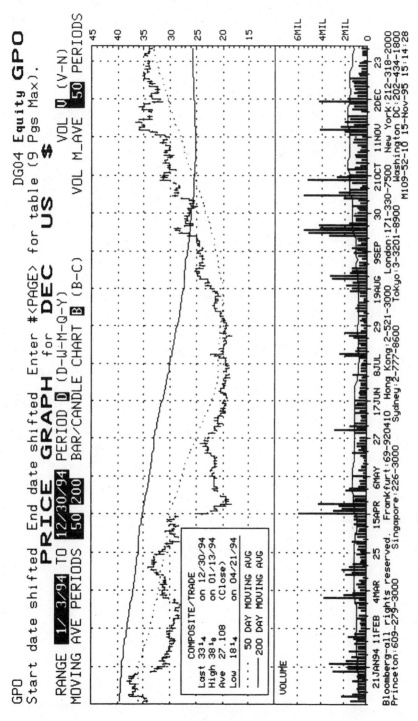

FIGURE 5-8 DEC low chart (1994). (*Courtesy of Bloomberg.*)

You will note the prominence of the planet Uranus (High Tech) in the Midheaven. In 1987, Transiting South Node conjunct Jupiter, plus Pluto in hard aspect to the Uranus and Midheaven, among others. In 1994, in contrast, we had more promising configurations, such as Jupiter conjunct the North Node, and the bottom being closed-timed by transiting Saturn square the natal Mars. To non-astrologers I realize this may sound a bit strange. But just mention these two sets of aspects to an astrology friend and ask which is considered the most and least favorable. Yes, you guessed it, the first was a top and the second a bottom!

Lucky Stars or Star-crossed Stocks?

As with so many star-crossed deals of the 1980s between the Americans and the Japanese, the Rockefeller Center sale was built on great arrogance and an inflated view of value. I like to point to this example, because as Warren Buffet says, "When you're buying stocks you're buying a company." And it can be a great company, just as RCP (Rockefeller Center Properties) has a great location, but it can be overpriced, as we said at the time. Many who bought real estate in the 1980s have still not recouped their initial investment. So look to value as well as to whether the company is good—at some point it is overvalued. See "Netscape" in Chapter 8 for a further discussion of this.

Mutual Funds

One of the newer factors affecting market behavior today is the proliferation of mutual funds. For example, in 1994 there were over 3600 funds, while by early 1995 there were over 5500—more than there are stocks listed on the New York Stock Exchange!

There are many very good reasons for the popularity of mutual funds today. They allow small investors some of the benefits previously available only to a privileged few. Investing in mutual funds

1. Gives you access to a professional money manager
2. Allows for diversification of stock risk
3. Allows for the playing of planetary themes with low-cost/no-cost industry-group switching
4. Easy access to global and emerging markets

Another reason mutual funds are popular is that they fit very well with a dollar-cost-averaging strategy. Adding $100 a month when buying an expensive stock could net you one share after commission, and a poor execution. Yet buying into a mutual fund family can give you ownership of blue chip stocks, which tend to enhance longer-term growth and the stability of one's portfolio at an acceptable cost. Another important benefit is less work. One doesn't have to spend time choosing the best individual stocks to own. It also isn't necessary to have the skill or inclination to study how economic forces and financial markets may affect specific stocks. Knowing your favorite style(s)—large caps, small caps, growth, value, international, contrarian, bond fund—can be sufficient.

With over 6000 mutual funds in existence, one can easily be tailored to a geographic region, individual country, and/or industry-group choice. They offer the individual investor many of the benefits previously available only to large money managers. Where possible check out the horoscope incorporation of a fund, listing data, and/or the birth data of the current fund manager(s).

Such a wide variety of choices is possible with mutual funds that some investors no longer see the need to buy individual stocks, but simply buy and sell funds. For example if one wanted to invest very conservatively or defensively, one could choose between numerous types of bond funds: municipal and government, corporate, international, etc., and if deemed appropriate, also metal and utility funds.

In addition to long-term performance, I also find it valuable to note the up- and down-market performance of a fund. This may be related to its Jupiter (up) and Saturn (down) astrological placements.

One piece of advice probably different from what you might expect: Rather than being over-concerned with the historical performance of a mutual fund, you may prefer to invest in a new one that has a favorable horoscope. Also, since performance varies greatly with different market conditions, I recommend investing in a fund specializing in an appropriate *upcoming* planetary theme. Past performance may be based on attunement to past planetary themes. Remember that today's winners can easily turn into tomorrow's laggards, if your investments are not finely attuned to the cosmos! Unfortunately, none of the major ranking services include this information—yet.

I would like to point out there is also an astrological basis for the viewpoint that one should invest in funds with long-standing positive records. The standard reason is that the fund manager has been tested over more than one market cycle. Astrologically, funds with over a seven-year track record have been tested by at least one Saturn Square—I refer to the famous seven-year itch. If it has outperformed during this time it is reasonable to assume that is because it has a strong natal birth chart and would be an appropriate vehicle for long-term investment.

A Gold Fund Example

Gold Funds generally are defensive in nature, and can be used to hedge a portfolio. For example they tend to do well in times of inflation, which is contrary to most other stock groups. Often this is a better strategy for many investors than buying naked puts.

Thus in 1996 and 1997, whenever the DJIA is above 5000, buying gold, gold stocks, and gold funds will be part of our hedging strategy for most investors.

Closed versus Open Funds

A closed fund does *not* allow for the inflow of new capital. Thus it may *not* be affected by market downturns in the same way as open funds, which when redeemed can force selling by the fund manager. It can also be a more "pure" astrological play, as the chart of the closed fund is of more relative importance than that of an open fund, which can theoretically be more greatly affected by the general market. Interestingly, closed funds may represent a premium or discount to the NAV (net asset value), if liquidated. Generally this presents an opportunity for extra profit, by buying a fund at a discount or selling it at a premium. However, this isn't always the case. I do recommend the first procedure *only* when there are clear *positive* astrological forecasts for the group or country. Even more so I recommend shorting the latter, but only when there are clear, very strong negative signals, as otherwise you could be fighting a very popular trend.

Again, if one is a long-term investor, one can simply buy one of each type of major fund: one large cap, one small cap, one bond, one growth, one value, one international, to *index* the market just as an index fund would do. This is a conservative approach, but one that I believe ignores some of the benefits of employing financial astrology. Next one could choose from a larger universe by including, when astrological indicators are favorable, such specialized funds as science and technology or gold.

Astrologically, one could diversify by buying into 12 funds, each incorporated in a different month. Theoretically one could buy those with Jupiter in the same sign and trine signs, and reduce exposure to those for Saturn in the same or trine sign. While this approach is a little simplistic it may have merit, and will be reproduced in a study due out this next year on our website. In the meantime here are three first-listing groups of mutual funds, in case you would like to investigate and/or purchase your-own-sign mutual fund!

The *Investors Business Daily* Mutual Fund Index List

Aries fund:	Franklin Growth, 3/31/48
	Gabelli Growth, 4/10/87
	Merrill Lynch Growth B, 3/27/87
Taurus fund:	Aim Aggressive Growth, 5/1/84
	Fidelity Contra, 5/17/67

	Janus Twenty, 4/26/85
	Skyline Special Equity, 4/23/87
	Fidelity Magellan, 5/2/63
Gemini fund:	Acorn Fund, 6/10/70
	Putnam Voyager, 6/1/69
Cancer fund:	CGM Capital Development, 6/22/61
	Scudder Capital Growth, 6/26/56
Leo fund:	Berger 100, 8/01/66
	IDS New Dimension, 7/30/68
Virgo fund:	Founders Special, 9/7/61
Libra fund:	
Scorpio fund:	Alger Small Cap, 11/11/86
	Twentieth Century Ultra, 11/2/81
Sagittarius fund:	
Capricorn fund:	Strong Opportunity, 12/31/85
Aquarius fund:	John Hancock Spec Equity, 2/4/85
Pisces fund:	PIMCO Opportunity C, 2/24/84

Note: Rather interesting that the oldest, i.e., first, fund listed is an Aries. No surprise to astrologers!

Morningstar Five-star Funds, and Higher-risk Stocks and Mutual Funds

Aries fund:	State Street Research Capital C (3/25/84)
Taurus fund:	
Gemini fund:	Putnam Voyager A (6/1/69)
Cancer fund:	Fidelity Select Develop Commun (6/29/90)
	Fidelity Select Health Care (7/14/81)
Leo fund:	Quantitative Numeric Ord (8/1/92)
Virgo fund:	Putnam New Opp A (8/31/90)
Libra fund:	T-Rowe Price Science & Technology (9/30/87)
Scorpio fund:	Quantitative Numeric Ord (11/1/82)
	Parkstone Small Cap Institl (10/31/88)
	Alger Growth (11/11/86)
Sagittarius fund:	20th Century Gift-Trust Inv (11/25/83)

Brandywine (12/12/85)

Capricorn fund: Invesco Strat Leisure (1/19/84)

MFS Emerging Growth B (12/29/86)

Fidelity Growth Company (1/17/83) HRS

Aquarius fund:

Pisces fund: Dimco Adv Opportunity C (2/24/84)

Morningstar Five-star Funds and Lower-risk Stocks and Mutual funds

Aries fund: Franklin Balance Sheet Investment (4/21/90)

Taurus fund: Robertson Stephens Value & Growth (5/12/92)

T-Rowe Price Mid Cap Growth (5/1/86)

Taurus Ventere (4/26/85)

Gemini fund:

Cancer fund: T-Rowe Price Mid Cap Growth (6/30/92)

Leo fund: Oakmark (8/5/91)

Fidelity Equity Income II (8/21/90)

Fidelity Select Food & Agriculture (7/29/85)

Pioneer Capital Growth A (7/25/90)

Virgo fund: Mutual Qualified (9/16/80)

Libra fund:

Scorpio fund: Lazard Small Cap (10/30/91)

Sagittarius fund:

Capricorn fund: Fidelity Blue Chip Growth (12/31/87)

Fidelity Low-Priced Stock (12/27/89)

Strong Common Stock (12/31/89)

Royce Premier (12/31/91)

Royce Micro-Cap (12/31/91)

Aquarius fund:

Pisces fund:

Note the unusually high percentage of low-risk stock mutual funds that are earth signs (Taurus, Virgo, Capricorn), which as a rule are more conservative. Again, no surprise to astrologers.

Astrological Guidelines for Trading

Money Management

In the days when I was a neophyte trader, I never left home without my QuoTrek, my portable stock market information quote machine. This is a practice I later regretted. Today I believe an active day trader should either watch a trading screen religiously or simply not trade, period. Market watching takes concentration, which is best left undivided. This is not to say, however, that entering a short-term trade by price limit cannot also be a successful strategy, and watching it only end-of-day with a modest stop. But I digress.

While staring at my QuoTrek in an elevator, a stranger inquired, "Is that a computer game you're playing?" I thought about this for a moment. "Yes," I replied, "it is." Indeed, and what a game! It is played by millions and millions of people, and at times watched by billions. It is played by both amateurs and professionals on an apparently but not really quite level playing field. There are no handicaps for poor players, as in golf. The main event begins at 9:30 A.M. Eastern Time, every Monday morning in New York. Intermission takes place at 4 P.M. and then proceeds each weekday morning until Friday, when all the players take off for a weekend holiday. Of course that's just one contest. Other games begin and end at different times around the world. Some, like currencies trading, are virtually 24-hour, seven-day-a-week game, with nary a rest period. Some of the games, like the futures game centered primarily in Chicago, are zero-sum games; that is, for every winner there is a loser. Others, like the New York game, are more egalitarian, as it's possible there to have both win-win and lose-lose scenarios. The main point is that as in every game, what wins is a combination of *luck and skill*. The more you know about the game, the better your chances are of winning. And as in all contests, whether sporting contests, horse racing, or market games, we note the starting time(s) to get astrological clues about the winners!

The single most important resource is *money*. The game called Wall Street is a much easier game to play with a lot of money than with a little. It is quite interesting that while almost all professional players believe it is difficult to play and takes a lot of hard work to win, they also compete against many amateurs who believe it is relatively easy to play and make money. How? The answer is simple, of course: *Simply buy low and sell high!* The more experienced may have a few extra guidelines like: *Let profits run, cut losses early, Don't add to a loser, Never marry a loser, Don't let a profit turn into a loss,* etc. One can even build up a simple mechanical trading system with such rules. While following them will not ensure that you make all the money in the world, they will at least allow you to keep playing the game longer—something your broker will appreciate!

Of course, if it were so simple to win the game known as Wall Street, almost all brokers and professional financial consultants would be rich, and we know that isn't the case. How come?

First, because you need lots of money to make lots of money. *Second,* because you need the right horoscope. *Third,* because Wall Street is not an easy, simple game.

Of course it is possible to make a lot of money with a little, but usually this involves much greater risk. Using astrology can reduce that risk somewhat, but if you believe *anyone* who tells you they can repeatedly win at trading, constantly pyramiding small capital into incredible heights, ask yourself: "Why does he [she] want *my* $5000 or $10,000?" Altruism? Of course, if you have not yet been burned by a bad experience, you may wish to invest in my prospective Brooklyn Bridge

REIT (Real Estate Investment Trust)....I plan on selling the shares very cheap, but you must wait if you wish to invest in this offering. It can be made by prospectus only, and for some reason the SEC wants to see my ownership papers before they will allow me to sell shares to the public.

Skill and experience are two major non-astrological factors that influence the outcome of trading. I hope you will benefit from my experience in what follows, as some of the mistakes I describe were made more than once before the lesson was learned.

An Astrological Trading Program

Astrology is defined as "a mathematical psychology based on astronomy." Astrology, i.e., psychology and timing, is viewed by an astrological analyst as a third force, along with the fundamental and technical factors that influence market behavior. An astrological analyst studies market behavior primarily by correlating planetary cycles with historical futures, options, and equities pricing. In forecasting overall market trends, the astrological analyst studies primarily the geocentric and heliocentric planetary patterns and their relationship to the horoscopes of various equity and futures market horoscopes.

I cannot say too often that while astrological factors should influence trading decisions, I strongly advocate that other factors such as market fundamentals and technical price movements also be taken into account in forecasting market fluctuations. When determining overall market trends, I also recommend that you check the state of your own personal chart. The timing of specific transactions utilizes astrological timing as a major factor in determining the best time of day to make purchases and sales for trading purposes. Knowledge of the horoscopes of various countries, world bourses, and currency charts should also play a major role in buying and selling stocks, bonds, futures, and options. Non-astrological factors such as one's knowledge of the stock market and one's ability to analyze the reports of various market analysts, as well as one's "market sense and feel" will also play a major role

in determining which financial instruments are to be pur-
chased. That being said, I personally rely primarily on my
expertise in financial astrology when forecasting trading.

Create more *profitable* solutions to some of your toughest
forecasting problems with Financial Astrology?

Astrology Trading Rules

One of the interesting properties of Wall Street and similar
market games is the fact that they constantly change and
evolve. This has to do not only with the use of supercomputers, mutual funds, hedge funds, derivatives, increased globalization of markets, and so forth, but also with astrology. The
sky is constantly changing, and this corresponds to changing
markets.

Know your horoscope is the first rule of astrology. It applies
to all the horoscopes you work with, starting with the most
important one, your own. Yet the first rule of finance is *know
your pocketbook*. Each person must combine these two rules
of financial astrology into a unique combination of the "right"
trading rules and best money management ideas. This must be
discovered for yourself, as we noted in Chapter 3. Different
systems work for different psychological (astrological) types.
You can use and develop dozens or even hundreds of trading
rules. My personal favorites follow. While they are always
uppermost in my mind, they should not be considered exhaus-
tive or complete, by any means.

Rule #1: Choose the Right Time

As a discretionary astrological trader and investor, rule number one *is* fundamental to astrological trading. This applies to
personal horoscope cycles, as we have frequently emphasized,
as well as to the horoscope(s) of your prospective purchases
and sales.

When you're hot, you're hot. When you're not, trade less,
research, and/or take a vacation from trading. One money
manager made an interesting proposal last year along these

lines. He suggested putting together a group of top financial astrologers and putting the one with the best horoscope cycle for each day in charge of making trading decisions for that day. This has yet to be done, but I fully support the concept.

One mistake that beginning traders often make is to over-trade. Rather than waiting patiently for the right moment to strike, they feel they need to be in the market almost at all times. My advice: "Be like a cat waiting for a mouse. Watch—wait—and *pounce*." Astrologically speaking it isn't advisable to trade every minute of the day, because of varying intraday astrological indicators.

Rule #2: Choose the Right Instruments

Being right about the market's direction won't guarantee you profitable trading. Naturally it helps, in that it is a *necessary* but not a *sufficient* cause of wealth building. Almost equal in importance is the choice of the proper trading instruments. Buying a far-out-of-the-money put or call option requires a *big* market move in order to make money. Thus an accurate market call about direction can lose money if there isn't sufficient precision. Don't unduly handicap yourself. Too often you get what you pay for, in that cheap options may become much more expensive to own in the long run because they so often lose money. Astrology helps, of course, but rarely do the markets move so dramatically.

An important corollary to Rule #2 is *diversify and weight*. On a purely astrological basis we can expect to be right better than 7 out of 10 times. (Of course, when combined with technical and other factors, the odds may improve somewhat.) We have found that trading five markets allows us sufficient diversification and profitability. Also, not all market calls are equal. Therefore we weight our calls in a one- to three-unit fashion. This allows differentiation between a 10-point DJIA move (P1 call) and a limit move of 50 points (P3). Each market has its own parameters, as do other trading systems. The important point is to differentiate among calls by weighting the size of the trade placed.

CALL WEIGHTING	DJIA (DOW)	SP 500
P1	10–25 points	100–250
P2	25–50 points	250–500
P3	50+ points	500+

Note that these numbers change with different market conditions. The important points to remember are that not all calls have equal weight, and to play stronger calls with more emphasis.

Rule #3: Choose the Right Money Management

This rule, concerned with how to take profits and losses, is a subject important enough to take up a whole book by itself. The following points I have found valid through personal experience. Unfortunately, despite having read about them in various books, I learned them all the hard way, from personal experience. Still, according to the old saw: "Only a fool makes the same mistake twice, while a wise man learns from the mistakes of others." A corollary here states:

> When in doubt, don't. When in, and in doubt, get out or set a tight stop.

One of the major advantages of using financial astrology is that it can provide you with a road map of *expected* market action. Thus when acting as a positional trader, I am not concerned if a small contrary trend is forecast. I am *very* concerned when (1) it lasts longer than it should, or (2) it is stronger than it was forecast to be.

Of the greatest concern are those times when the market is not acting as I had believed (forecast) it should. This period of doubting should *never* be an active period. I believe in planned trades. This explains how, even in the midst of a wild market, I can act confidently. But remember, if you have no desire to stand in front of a freight train, that these trades should not go contrary to the apparent secular trend. I also use a rule of thumb that they must be planned in advance. It may just be my natural contrarian nature at work, but disaster could otherwise follow. Extreme caution is called for, unless one is backed up by good technical trading signals. Here's another corollary:

Don't trade what you won't invest.

Which has its *own* corollary:

Don't confuse day trading with position trading.

Like all rules, this one has some notable exceptions. But when trading stocks short-term, I rarely recommend buying or shorting a stock even for an intraday trade, unless it's a position I'd be willing to hold long(er)-term.

Put another way, I prefer directional confirmation from either my intermediate- or long-term trading view *with* my short-term trade. Yes, one can trade both ways, and I used to do more of this when I first started trading. Now I more often use the expected countertrend move in the way my mentors first tried to teach me to do, simply as an entry point.

EXPECTED MOVE	INTERMEDIATE VIEW	RECOMMENDED ACTION
Two handles up	Up	Buy
Two handles down	Down	Sell
Two handles up	Down	Wait, then sell
Two handles down	Up	Wait, then buy

An example here would be if I am a strong market bear but am expecting a two-handle (200 points SP) upside move first. Rather than automatically playing the upside, I wait until the move is near-complete and short what I believe is the top. The reason for this caution is clear. Sometimes a larger wave will come and destroy a minor countertrend trade. Nothing hurts more, emotionally and financially, than to be right about the big move and still lose money on a baby countertrend trade. I find the markets a sufficiently worthy opponent without having to play against *myself* in the bargain.

Of course if the countertrend move is very large, such as three or four handles or more, the trader in me often will want to play the upside first. Always this depends on the expected strength of the move. For example, a brief intraday move may be ignored, while a countertrend day may not. Again, ideally these indications should come from *both* astrology *and* technical signals. A corollary:

Watch the risk/reward ratio carefully.

There are many differing approaches to the risk/reward ratio. As a general rule of thumb, a 1:3 ratio is desirable. This means that I am willing to risk a $100 loss for a potential $300 gain. But this assumes at least a 50-50 chance of success, even up to 80 percent right. I use this for P1 calls. For P2 calls, 2:1, and for P3, 1:1. That is to say, with increasing certainty I am willing to day-trade small bets if the astrological odds are highly favorable. Again, the principle is more important than the numbering system, which can be adjusted to individual tastes and specific markets.

Risk reward ratio	Estimated probability	Strength of call
3:1	50% or better	P1
2:1	70% or better	P2
1:1	80% or better	P3

One very important part of the consideration is the use of stops. Volumes could be written on the subject, but let's just say I disagree with the prevalent view of the use of stops as being primarily a money management tool. Stops most often are used to help to preserve principal in trading. This is their secondary function. For example, if I begin with $1000, trade profitably seven times, and make an average of $100 each time, but lose $1700 in the eighth trade, I am broke. Trading with too little capital is a losing game. It's fine if you view the markets as an entertainment substitute for Las Vegas. Otherwise, consider carefully the time you must invest in trading: It should compensate you more than your present line of work. Otherwise, why trade? Better to work with a professional money manager.

How do I view stops? As the point in play at which I *am wrong* to continue holding my current position. If the market reaches my stop point, it is likely to go much *further* against me. Now one must also calculate whether one can afford the stop point that invalidates the trading position. If not, prudent money management says *don't enter into the play in the first place!*

Some most important questions to ask in professional trading are "What happens if I'm wrong? Can I afford the loss? Can I still make money?" A sufficiently astute trader (in contrast to a market caller/timer) has the knowledge to hedge positions by buying instruments that will positively outperform when correct and be hedged most of the time with only relatively small losses when not. As an example, be long bonds by a key support level, and short the SP near a strong resistance area. Can you follow why this strategy will work in different markets? By breaking even or often losing a little when wrong, this allows for greater overall profits when correct. If you don't follow me here, it may be a very good idea to find a broker or trading partner who does.

Profits and Losses

Rule #1: Protect profits; if you ignore your profits, they will just go away.

"Playing for the big score" is more than a dream for small players, it is their frequent nemesis. In my earlier days I often liked to play "options-expiration Friday." There were no real-time premiums, and for a few hundred dollars I had a unique opportunity to make money that was available only once a month. Often I would become convinced the market would break my way, and I wouldn't accept the double the market offered me for a few moments. While my trading partner took his profits, I held. Not surprisingly, I would frequently then lose it all by the end of the day. (*Note:* playing out of the money OEX puts/calls.)

Like almost all of my lessons, this one was brought home to me by an experience. You would think that by dint of frequent losses I would learn. Not so—I'm a fixed sign in astrology. But again, I had an astrological edge that allowed me to play longer, as the first entry most often was right.

I returned from a European vacation the day before one options-expiration Friday. Europe is of course much more long-term-oriented than America in its thinking. By eating the food and breathing the air, I somehow acquired a longer-term view. I entered a position, the market quickly doubled, I took my profits. Ironically, what happened? Unlike the previous nine option expirations, this was a *big one*. The initial position would have increased ten times! I soon realized this and reentered the position, and by market close had doubled my money a second time that day. The following realization was brought home: I was able to quadruple my money out of a maximum tenfold profit-day. But a tenfold profit-day is rare indeed, and perhaps happens only 1 time in 10. Had I taken my doubles every time, I would have been far better off. Playing like an amateur, I was afraid of missing the big one. But I learned that I would not lose out if I played prudently. That was a real eye-opener for me. This is why it is often said: *If you don't know yourself well, the market can be a very expensive place to learn.*

Rule #2: Reassess constantly.

The moment you would no longer freshly enter the same position, exit immediately, or place a tight stop order. Hope is a great enemy of traders. If *you* wouldn't buy the same stock at this current price, why should anybody else? People buy because they feel that the price in the future will be greater than at the present time. There should be no compromise here. The cost of commissions is now so relatively low that you can always reenter if you feel you made a mistake, or if your assessment of market conditions changes. *It doesn't matter what you paid.* I don't care if you have a profit or are holding a losing position. Just *act.* The famous wait, to "at least just get even," is the amateur's way of not admitting to a mistake.

Rule #3: Hold day trading positions overnight.

One great problem with day-trading in excess is that positions must be closed by the end of the market, regardless of how it will open the following day. Ideally there should be sufficient equity to hold all positions overnight if desired. But don't confuse day trading and position trading. If you are day trading and you don't expect to gain any appreciable advantage by staying overnight, exit your position. If you have no idea of the opening, due to a news report, or you feel there is significant risk that the market may open against you—don't hesitate, just exit your position. You can always reenter in the morning.

To summarize: When the horoscope(s) of the opening market(s) seem(s) favorable to your position, hold it overnight. When you are unsure, have no idea, or feel there is significant risk the market may open against your position, close it by the end of the day.

Rule #4: Call the last one-eighth, day-trade the last one-fourth, and position-trade the last one-half.

Theoretically, it is very satisfying emotionally to try to call the top or bottom of market moves. Financially, it is *very* unwise. Too many trades are lost by trying to stay to the very end of a move. The famous Wall Street trader Bernard Baruch was said to be happy to give the first and last 10 percent to others: "Don't try to buy at the bottom or sell at the top." He was quite happy with 80 percent of any market move. This sentiment is shared by almost all successful traders. On the other hand we have Paul Tudor Jones, one of the world's most successful futures traders, who recognizes that immense profits can be made if one knows how: "I believe the very best money is made at the market turns." Such can be the potential value of astrological trading.

In January 1989, my first month of trading options, I often was able to time the day a computer stock would jump. I kept refining my work, trying to precisely time the exact minute of a move. One particular option play was for Wyse computer, which at the time was selling for a little more than $6. I had a stopwatch handy and my broker on the phone, and I kept him waiting for a minute and a half. Then I said, "Buy." But before the time the option order could be filled the market had already moved, and Wyse was $8! (In those days the order was written up by hand, then sent to the floor—a total turnaround time of about 3 to 4 minutes. Today, of course, I have computer execution.) After living through several such scenarios, I no longer *play* the last one-eighth of any move, although I frequently do *call* it.

Playing against yourself is a zero-sum game. At times, like all traders, we astrologers are surprised by the markets. This could be due to an error in calculation, judgment, or data, or for any other reason. It doesn't matter. The fact is, we are wrong at times. As soon as a mistake is recognized, acknowledge it and *act*. Any delay usually is costly, and over the long haul you will lose.

Rule #5: Break any rule carefully, and be sure to have favorable horoscope indications when you do!

Note: For advanced traders, what doesn't work, *really* works.

STRONG RELIABLE INDICATOR	SHORT-TERM ACTION	NEXT MARKET MOVE
Big up	Flat, slightly up	Big down
Big down	Flat, slightly down	Big up

One of the most profitable indicators in *any* trading system is when it doesn't work. If we're expecting a big upside move and the market is stagnant, there's a major chance that a bigger, undiscovered, or uncharted cycle is about to explode. I admit I'm not always fast enough to exploit this. It's one of the few areas where I'm willing to concede that a computerized trading program can outperform me. Some of the biggest movements, and most profitable trades, stem from such failures of reliable indicators. Of course if the indicators aren't well tested or applied, we're not talking the same story.

Hot Stocks

In Chapter 7, we discuss—along with news—stock splits, company splits or spinoffs, and mergers and acquisitions that can be hot. Routinely, stocks often have risen on a stock split, followed by a fall. A company split usually occurs because shareholders don't believe they're getting full value, and often it is accompanied by an initial rise. With mergers the acquired company usually rises, whereas the acquiring one may fall. In the recent Chase/Chemical merger, well forecast by Bill Eng in his *Best Stocks to Trade for 1995*, both stocks rose, as the proposed deal made sense from the viewpoint of both companies.

Selecting stocks by looking at the exchange listing time corresponds to technical analysis. While, theoretically, price action should reflect a stock's fundamentals, often this is not the case. Bill Meridian popularized the concept of the first trade to account for much over- and undervaluation. My understanding is that Bill uses the first trade as a primary indicator, then backs it up through technicals and the incorporation chart.

In his book *Planetary Stock Trading*, Bill provides us with these six rules:

1. Select a small group of stocks to work with.
2. Select horoscopes that make soft or positive connections to your own.

3. Understand the concept of relative strength.

4. Trade with the trend; the trend is your friend.

5. Different groups of stocks have different characteristics.

6. Confirm selections through technical analysis.

I work the other way round, looking primarily at the incorporation chart and then backing it up by technicals and the first trade chart. Remember, I never like to trade a stock I want to invest in. In a similar vein, I usually won't play M&A games unless I believe the acquired stock is undervalued and would in time be worth the purchase price. Conversely, however, I am most happy to short the acquiring company if I don't care for the deal on fundamental and astrological grounds. Also, I'm willing to short the company to be acquired if its horoscope strongly suggests a failed acquisition or merger.

Shorting Stocks: When It's Raining, the Farmers Are Happy

Shorting or selling a stock first, then buying it back later, can be very risky, especially in bull markets. Two non-astrological rules to keep in mind: *Be wary of shorting a popular stock* (i.e., short with the winds with you, not against you) and *be wary of shorting a popular short,* or you could end up crushed in a short squeeze. Another point to remember if you short stock is that you are responsible for paying out any dividends. However, you aren't likely to short a high-dividend-yielding stock, as it is unlikely to be considered overvalued.

We will now look at DEC at two pivotal movements in time: its price action before the 1987 crash at just under 200, and its latest bottom. We can again view the same data through the lens of the DEC first trade chart (Fig. 6-1). Mars and Uranus are the astrological rulers of what is *hot* and *quick,* respectively.

In Fig. 6-2, I have used another popular technique that astrologers employ, that of the solar return chart. In the chart

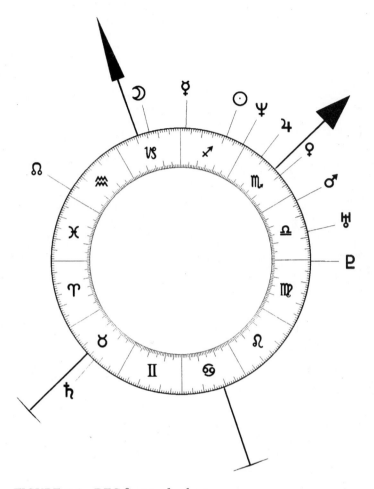

FIGURE 6-1   DEC first trade chart.

for 1987 Sun and Saturn are prominent, indicating a strong dose of hard reality. In the 1994 chart, the Sun is at the lowest point of the chart, showing the potentiality for a new cyclic upswing. In Fig. 6-3 we also see the next year's chart, and see the favorable Moon–Jupiter–Pluto on the Ascendant and Saturn at the lowest point of the chart, both again indicating a new cyclic upswing.

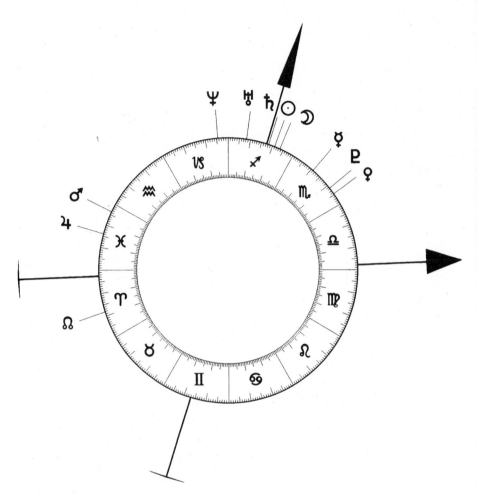

FIGURE 6-2   DEC first trade year (1987) chart.

Options and Futures

Many new option players are especially prone to the belief that the markets are designed to purposely frustrate the greatest number of players. For example, have you ever noticed that when you wish to *buy an option*, the price is always a bit on the high side; *sell an option*, the price is almost always on the low side; and when you finally *give up on a market play*, the stock market action you keep waiting to happen finally takes place?

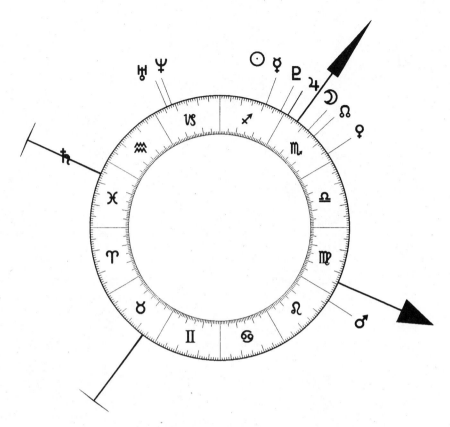

FIGURE 6-3   DEC first trade year (1995) chart.

ASTROLOGY AND OPTIONS	RESULT
Accurate timing	Making money
Precise timing	Losing less money if/when wrong

The key point about playing options and futures is not only
to be right, but to be right in *time*. To say that the market will
rise strongly in two or three months but be wrong by one day,
can be totally devastating. This premium on extremely precise
timing is why there are numerous successful traders who

incorporate astrological elements into their trading system or who consult astrologers.

A second equally important point is that astrology's capability to precisely time forecasts facilitates only a little time-premium loss for the trader. There are two costs of buying or selling an option: the intrinsic value and the time premium. Even when an astrological forecast is wrong, it can be so crafted as to cover only the very smallest selected segments of time. These cumulative time windows constitute an extremely important trading edge.

CYCLE	BEGINS	MOST IMPORTANT
Option cycle	Third Friday each month	March, June, Sept., Dec.
Calendar cycle	First of the month	April 1; July 1; October 1; Jan. 1
Solar cycle	21–23 of the month	March, June, Sept., Dec.
Lunation cycle	Monthly; rotates	Eclipses; various

I find the market pricing to be most realistic on options-expiration day. On that day market participants must exchange payment for derivative propositions. Of course the price of certain stocks may be skewed and rounded up or down to a strike price, so as to eliminate the need to pay out to a number of players. So we have many cycles to consider. During options-expiration week we need stronger indicators to play our P2 and P3 indicators. This is because there is a strong tendency to shake out the weaker players at this time. Market volatility increases dramatically. In addition the monthly option-expiration cycles, which are strongest quarterly, require our P3 indicators. We have monthly and quarterly calendar cycles, preceded by window-dressing money managers. Also, as fiscal compensation increasingly is tied to market performance, these cycles become increasingly important.

We also have two primary astrological cycles to chart: the monthly Solar cycle, when the Sun goes into Aries, Taurus, Gemini, etc., and the four most important Solstice and Equinox charts. Interestingly enough, these correspond to the four key quarterly option-expiration cycles. We also have the monthly Lunar Cycle, with the New Moon–Full Moon–New Moon cycle, punctuated by Solar and Lunar Eclipses at the time of the New Moon and the Full Moon, respectively. Market volatility also can increase during changes in these cycles as well, necessitating further confirmations or the stronger P2 and, in some cases, P3 trading signals and rules. All of these different monthly/quarterly cycles—Options, Calendar, Solar, Lunar—can be used to identify turning points in markets by looking at the astrological condition at work during key parts of the cycles. The important point to keep in mind is that the confluence of these overlapping cycles requires the strongest possible indicators before a position play can be recommended.

Of course if one is buying an option or future for hedging purposes, in contrast to speculation, that is a horse of a different color. Then we don't worry as much about the penalty for being wrong in dramatic markets, as our purchase is just for this reason. As with covered call writing, which is a conservative way to hedge against temporary market downdrafts, options and futures are played differently for hedging or speculation. In general we need stronger indications to play P2 and P3, because the penalty for being wrong is greater.

Again, I can't overstress that trading options and futures, like all high risk/reward ventures, should be traded *only* with risk capital. I define risk capital as money that you can afford to lose without any major change in your lifestyle.

Integrating Astrology with Technical Trading

Many technical traders are to a large extent open to the science of astrology, which they view as simply another form of charting. One insider estimates that at least 30 percent of the most successful market technicians incorporate (in secret) at least some element of astrology into their timing system. Perhaps he exaggerates, but anyway we both agree that they certainly *should* even if they don't.

Traders check astrological data before trading because

financial astrology

1. Offers trading signals not made available by other technical tools
2. Gives *earlier* trading signals
3. Integrates with intraday, daily, or longer-term trading

The point of integrating multiple trading systems or traders is to increase profitability. This is done primarily by increasing the reliability of trading signals. When two reliable systems agree, there is the greatest likelihood of success. But what about when they *disagree?* This can be tricky.

The trick is to filter out the losing trades without also filtering out an equivalent total of winning trades. "Total" here refers to profitability, not a numerical count. So if by adding a new element or rule to a trading system I eliminate three winning and two losing trades, that's fine so long as the net result is *more* profit. In general, what works best is to trade when both systems agree. Even then I find it best to trade only my strongest signals or recommend to a technical trader that he/she trade only the strongest. If both strongly disagree it is best to be sidelined, if your ego can handle it. If they disagree, I of course prefer astrological trading, while my technical trading partners prefers their signals. However, if the nature of the signal is a market-surprise signal, even my trading partners have learned how stiff is the penalty for not stepping outside of their own trading system and bowing to the will of the cosmos!

A claim can be made that technical analysis is merely a self-fulfilling prophecy. Certainly in the futures market especially, many technical trades are made by anticipating other technical traders. But as with astrology, there is a natural basis to it. For example the natural tendency of many amateurs is to "get even." To not take it personally means that even in the act of losing money you can admit that you were wrong. Professionals have little problem doing this. They just want to be right more often, i.e., make money. This is one key difference between amateurs and professionals. Many amateur futures players simply enjoy the game and play it for enjoyment, much like betting the races or playing roulette in Las Vegas. This is fine as long as the size of the betting is restricted to what the player can *easily* afford to lose.

Because the market is a combination of the two factors of Time and Price, I use a proprietary pricing model. It was developed over a two-year period by staring at a screen and gradually discovering some underlying principles. This is what happened to me. One morning I awoke early with "the answer," rushed to my office, and wrote up my "dream" discovery. It is a kind of mixture of classical numerology, W. D. Gann, and candlestick charting, although independently discovered. After all the truth is the truth, and clearly any fresh "new" system will show correspondences to previous ones. I also like to integrate my work with that of a few key associates whose opinion I have come to value over time. For example, why duplicate the work of a fine market technician if I can gain timely access to it, in exchange for granting him or her access to *my* work?

Again I would like to stress that a strong positive chart connection to a trading partner is highly desirable. If it's weak, then make sure you include other elements (charts) in the picture. A weak chart contact shouldn't be your primary partner, for even if good by him/herself, he/she won't supply you with what you need. Every time I broke this rule, I lost money or clients.

Trending, or Trading the Markets

One of the more useful things one can do is to determine whether a market is in a *trending* or a *trading* mode. A trending market is one that continues a large up or down movement over time. A trading market moves sideways, often reversing direction at key support and resistance areas. In a trending market, such areas are penetrated.

While I don't have a single astrological tool that accomplishes this, a number of background indicators often are present. For example, a large number of alternating mixed signals often can appear in trading markets, while multiple indicators of the same direction would correspond to a trending market. Consider the three primary planets of price movement in both markets, Jupiter, Saturn, and Pluto. Obviously a Saturn time or down signal at resistance, or Jupiter time or up signal at support, will lend credence to a trading market. Conversely Jupiter at resistance, or Saturn at support, will facilitate the breakout of a trend, i.e., if the trend is a sufficiently strong (P2 or P3) indicator.

Pluto	Support	Trending	Breakout down
Pluto	Support	Trading	Up
Pluto	Resistance	Trending	Breakout up
Pluto	Resistance	Trading	Down

Pluto action is somewhat different, and acts somewhat like a stochastic indicator. In a trending market, Pluto will break out of *both* support and resistance. In a trading market, Pluto reverses market direction at support and resistance points. Hence the great importance of determining overall market conditions.

News and Geopolitical "Surprises"

Correctly anticipated market "surprises" are among the most lucrative endeavors for financial astrologers. Dramatic profits can be accrued when one anticipates an unanticipated economic report number. But remember: *The markets hate surprises.* Financial markets can turn on a dime when surprised. Conversely, or perhaps *perversely*, the market often will shrug off a horrible news report if it had been expected. Analysts already had factored it into their calculations.

MARKET EXPECTATION	SURPRISE EXPECTED?	ACTION
Positive	Yes	Sell
Negative	Yes	Buy

Earning surprises, when the profits or losses differ significantly from what brokerage houses expect, are of two types, positive and negative. The negative earning surprise can have a devastating impact on the price of a stock. Conversely, a positive new surprise usually results in an increase in stock price. However, when highly positive earnings are expected, this may trigger widespread selling. The key question to ask before viewing a scheduled news report is "Is the available news I foresee built into the market price?"

Equally dramatic in effect, especially in the currency markets, can be surprise interest-rate shifts by the Big Four central banks: the Federal Reserve Bank, Bank of England, German Bundesbank, and the Bank of Japan. Corporate earning "surprises," "surprise" takeover bids, and corporate disasters also are not always surprise events to financial astrologers. We estimate that financial astrologers are truly surprised by market "surprises" only about half of the time.

News reports consist of two types, scheduled and unscheduled. Most scheduled reports tend to be released at either 8:30 or 10 A.M. One can do a horoscope for the time a report is to be released. Accordingly one looks to check the "look and feel" of the chart. Does it agree with the analysts' consensus? From a trading perspective, does it reflect what the market is anticipating at the close of the day before? For if the news *we* are expecting is also what *others* are expecting, little profit is to be hoped for. If on the other hand we believe the consensus view to be wrong on fundamental grounds, and the news report horoscope agrees with us, it is generally worthwhile to take a contrarian position. Additionally, because a contrarian view is already expected, even if we are wrong, there may be little penalty for overnight entry. This is especially the case when the news report is anticipated to be strongly positive or negative.

Another type of news story is a scheduled meeting of the Big Four central banks, such as at a FOMC meeting. Our most celebrated forecast in 1994 was of the Federal Reserve Board's reversal of interest rates in early February. From an astrological point of view, that was a no-brainer. I remember being called by one of the news services several months later, regarding a rumor that Orange County Treasurer Robert Citron was using astrology. "Not very likely," I stated. "And if he was," I added, "his astrologer should be fired for incompetence or sloppy work in transposing the U.S. and Japanese horoscopes! (In case you don't remember this disaster, Treasurer Citron was aggressively using derivatives in his management of that conservative county's tax funds. He was betting that interest rates not only would stay low but get lower. In 1994, this bet lost Orange County, California, $2 billion of its $7.4 billion investment portfolio.)

Another type of news story occurs when a company holds its annual meeting or schedules a news conference, such as for the release of a product, or releases it quarterly earning results. Again we try to find an extreme divergence, whenever possible. Only in these cases we are relating the time (as known) of the meeting or press release to the horoscope of the company. We do know of a few companies that pay astrologers to choose the time of news conferences. Why bother? Isn't bad news bad news? Not necessarily. *How* something is taken is, to a surprising extent, reflected in the horoscope time. To me, the ABCs of corporate damage control are

A. Admit the problem quickly.

B. Outline steps to be taken to remedy the problem.

C. Release this news to the press at an astrologically appropriate moment!

IBM

At one time, IBM was king of the mountain. To make a major market move without considering IBM was unthinkable. Yet due to a number of strategic errors, especially in the PC arena, it fell from grace. This bluest of blue chips not only broke 100 in July 92, but then broke 50 to go to a low of 40⅝ in August of 1993. (See also Fig. 7-1.) Somewhere, support had to be found. We strongly believed that it would again climb up to above 100. Why? Because all of the bad news was already built in: mainframe sales were declining, operating costs were higher than the industry average, the IBM trademark was no longer a magic name, etc. Therefore one looked for positive news, for positive news surprises. Looking at the Solar Return (yearly birthday horoscopes) in 1994, 1995 (see Fig. 7-2), and 1996, we saw a change toward an upswing.

Why weren't many other analysts surprised? When we stated on CNN January 1, 1995, that IBM would climb past 100 by midyear, the newscaster's face reflected shock and disbelief. IBM again at 100? Impossible. Later, IBM's quarterly earnings were more than double what most analysts had been

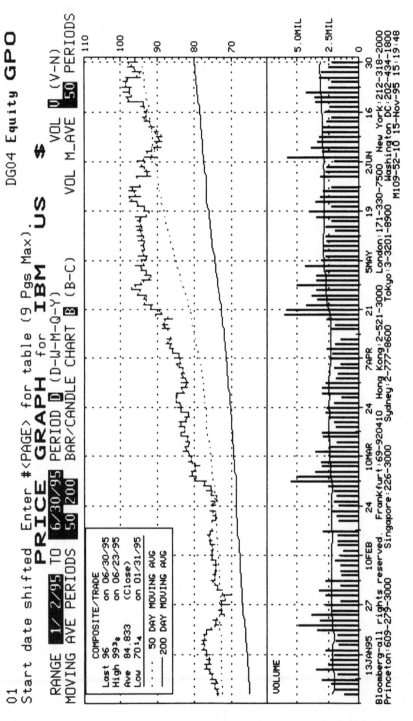

FIGURE 7-1 IBM technical chart, 1995. (*Courtesy of Bloomberg.*)

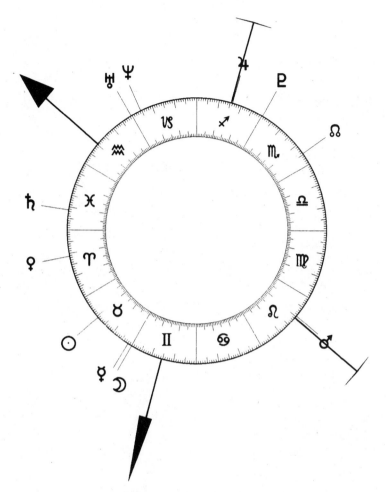

FIGURE 7-2 IBM horoscope chart, 1995.

expecting. This surprise helped to fuel an upward move. So IBM wasn't dead, after all! But *why* were so many people surprised? *Why* weren't they checking IBM's horoscope? Didn't they see the angular Mars–Jupiter success aspect prominent, as we did?

We have already discussed the fact that political events, such as elections, influence markets. Geopolitical events such as crises caused by military coups, political shakeouts, and earthquakes and other natural disasters also influence market behavior. As you would expect, there is an astrological correlation to such crises. The Chinese character for *crisis* is made up of two pictograms: one for *danger,* the other for *opportunity.* A discussion of a few world crises and the subsequent market opportunities follows.

In January of 1991 I was informed by one of Russia's leading astrologers to expect severe political problems in the former Soviet Union in the third or fourth week of August. He intimated that a major government shake-up and coup was in the offering. As time went on, I simply forgot about his prediction. But on August 24 the newspaper headlines screamed of the coup attempt on Gorbachev. One market effect was seen in the grain markets. They reacted to the news violently, as the new leaders of Russia were hard-liners and not thought to be friendly to the West. All previously signed contracts with the government of Russia might well be reneged upon. Having in my possession a copy of Gorbachev's horoscope, we did a quick study and were able to send out press releases stating categorically, "This coup will be over in three days." We also recommended taking positions in the grain futures market for the first time. These proved to be extremely profitable recommendations. Quite a good *coup,* if you'll excuse the pun, and a relatively simple one for astrologers. That is, if you had the right chart, and if you were *looking.*

We have stated that astrologers also are often surprised by markets, if less frequently than others. Buy why are they surprised at all? There are many reasons for this. First, they may not have been looking. So far we have only talked about anticipated surprises. Potentially there are thousands of horoscopes that could be studied. Remember that there are horoscopes for every country, world leader, stock market, stock, etc. Years ago all this would have been an impossible task. Today it might be possible to examine all those horoscopes by employing the massively high-speed supercomputers, running parallel processing. But even with all "perfect" techniques, there will be surprises. Assuming ample computer resources, one still is left with the problem of data veracity: All horoscope dates would have to be tested so as to be valid. This problem of bad data is dealt with in Appendix II.

My working hypothesis is that the planets act as a *trigger effect*. A certain amount of energy or force applied at just the right time or place (like a fulcrum) greatly magnifies an ordinary effect. I don't believe that the planets "cause" events, but when the proper background conditions are present, they can *trigger* them. Thus when predicting a market surprise, one needs to assess a great amount of in-depth and current information about economics, politics, etc. Yes, it is possible to forecast in astrology blindly, i.e., without knowledge of the particulars, but this gives less precise results.

Remember, financial astrology is a co-specialty field. Clearly when a situation is potentially expected, as the Japanese market crash was, and one just wants to know "when," this becomes a relatively easy task with standard astrological charting. Events then prove us right or wrong. As I have often advised: "If you don't have the required expertise, outsource it." Find a trading partner with the required expertise, or develop sources of information that help to supplement yours.

Of course, most of the time "surprise" events are by definition not anticipated. How then can we predict them? For example, if Mexico is having a Mars–Pluto aspect to its Sun, will it result in riots or violence? Will it correspond to a large volcanic eruption? Will it be a non-event? Or will a financial astrologer working for the Mexican government mitigate its effect and work with the cosmos? In the future this will no more be a farfetched concept than an attempt by government economists to smooth out the business cycle. Today this is where the skill and experience of a financial astrologer can truly make a critical difference.

Again, even given every possible surprise event, the market may *not* turn on a dime. As an analogy, consider a person suffering from ill health and poor astrological aspects. The moment when more positive, healing astrological influences are felt does not usually bring on "instant" healing. It takes time to recover full health.

And here, finally, we have a unique astrological explanation for why astrologers sometimes are surprised by markets.

Uranus in astrology is the planet of "surprises." By definition, it *will* surprise. Thus an astrologer quickly learns in practice that when Uranus is strong, he or she should advise clients that forthcoming events aren't likely to be what one might expect.

For example when Uranus, the planet of surprises and earthquakes, went over the Midheaven of the Japanese chart, we were expecting an "expected" earthquake. (See Fig. 7-3.) We were somewhat surprised, for what came was not the big

Search From Jan 1, 1990 to Jan 1, 2000
Hits: 25 (Maximum: 2600)
Natal Chart: JAPAN
Greenwich, ENG. GMT +00:00
000W00'00" 051N30'00"
Tropical Zodiac
Geocentric

Transit to Natal
Search Planets: -- -- -- -- -- -- Ur -- Pl --
Target Planets: Mo Su Me Ve Ma Ju Sa Ur Ne Pl No Mc As -- -- -- -- -- -- -- -- -- -- -- -- -- -- -- -- -- --
Aspect Set: Conjunction
Aspects: CNJ
Find: Aspects

Aspect	Date	Time	Event	Type	Natal Chart	P1 Pos.	P2 Pos
⯓ ---- ☌ Mc	04-18-1990	08:35 am	⯓ ☌ Mc	Tr-Na	JAPAN	16°♏55'℞	16°♏55'
⯓ ---- ☌ Mc	05-24-1990	05:29 pm	⯓ ☌ Mc	Tr-Na	JAPAN	15°♏55'℞	16°♏55'
⯓ ---- ☌ Mc	09-22-1990	11:16 pm	⯓ ☌ Mc	Tr-Na	JAPAN	15°♏55'	16°♏55'
⯓ ---- ☌ Mc	10-21-1990	12:37 pm	⯓ ☌ Mc	Tr-Na	JAPAN	16°♏55'	16°♏55'
⯓ ---- ☌ Mc	11-15-1990	01:37 pm	⯓ ☌ Mc	Tr-Na	JAPAN	17°♏55'	16°♏55'
⯓ ---- ☌ Mc	06-22-1991	12:23 pm	⯓ ☌ Mc	Tr-Na	JAPAN	17°♏55'℞	16°♏55'
⯓ ---- ☌ Mc	09-02-1991	09:20 am	⯓ ☌ Mc	Tr-Na	JAPAN	17°♏55'	16°♏55'
⯓ ---- ☌ ♃	11-22-1992	10:31 am	⯓ ☌ ♃	Tr-Na	JAPAN	23°♏10'	24°♏10'℞
⯓ ---- ☌ ♃	12-18-1992	04:11 pm	⯓ ☌ ♃	Tr-Na	JAPAN	24°♏10'	24°♏10'℞
⯓ ---- ☌ ♃	01-22-1993	09:40 pm	⯓ ☌ ♃	Tr-Na	JAPAN	25°♏10'	24°♏10'℞
⯓ ---- ☌ ♃	04-03-1993	12:53 pm	⯓ ☌ ♃	Tr-Na	JAPAN	25°♏10'℞	24°♏10'℞
⯓ ---- ☌ ♃	05-14-1993	00:34 am	⯓ ☌ ♃	Tr-Na	JAPAN	24°♏10'℞	24°♏10'℞
⯓ ---- ☌ ♃	06-22-1993	11:36 am	⯓ ☌ ♃	Tr-Na	JAPAN	23°♏10'℞	24°♏10'℞
⯓ ---- ☌ ♃	09-11-1993	06:47 pm	⯓ ☌ ♃	Tr-Na	JAPAN	23°♏10'	24°♏10'℞
⯓ ---- ☌ ♃	10-16-1993	00:31 am	⯓ ☌ ♃	Tr-Na	JAPAN	24°♏10'	24°♏10'℞
⯓ ---- ☌ ♃	11-11-1993	06:06 am	⯓ ☌ ♃	Tr-Na	JAPAN	25°♏10'	24°♏10'℞
♅ ---- ☌ Asc	03-17-1994	03:13 pm	♅ ☌ Asc	Tr-Na	JAPAN	25°♑32'	26°♑32'
♅ ---- ☌ Asc	06-15-1994	08:45 pm	♅ ☌ Asc	Tr-Na	JAPAN	25°♑32'℞	26°♑32'
♅ ---- ☌ Asc	01-02-1995	03:04 am	♅ ☌ Asc	Tr-Na	JAPAN	25°♑32'	26°♑32'
♅ ---- ☌ Asc	01-19-1995	03:51 am	♅ ☌ Asc	Tr-Na	JAPAN	26°♑32'	26°♑32'
♅ ---- ☌ Asc	02-05-1995	07:59 am	♅ ☌ Asc	Tr-Na	JAPAN	27°♑32'	26°♑32'
♅ ---- ☌ Asc	08-15-1995	04:17 pm	♅ ☌ Asc	Tr-Na	JAPAN	27°♑32'℞	26°♑32'
♅ ---- ☌ Asc	10-01-1995	06:48 am	♅ ☌ Asc	Tr-Na	JAPAN	26°♑32'℞	26°♑32'
♅ ---- ☌ Asc	10-11-1995	05:21 pm	♅ ☌ Asc	Tr-Na	JAPAN	26°♑32'	26°♑32'
♅ ---- ☌ Asc	11-25-1995	00:21 am	♅ ☌ Asc	Tr-Na	JAPAN	27°♑32'	26°♑32'

FIGURE 7-3 **"Earthquake" chart for Japan. Note the Pluto conjunct Jupiter; transformation (Pluto) of the rulers (Jupiter). Also note Uranus ascendant, a classic earthquake aspect.**

Kobe quake that arrived later, but a *political* earthquake that shook up the ruling LDP party and greatly unsettled the post-war Japanese political order. It could be argued that a more thorough examination of the Japanese charts, and greater expertise on the part of the author, would have produced a more authentic result. Perhaps in an ideal world it would have, but we got the market result we were looking for at the right time, and accordingly were satisfied.

Special Situations

The selection of venture capital and IPO candidates are among the most profitable venues for financial astrology. Quite a number of newly issued shares have had most stellar starts, gaining more than 100 percent in price *the very first day*. This growing list includes Netscape Communications, Boston Chicken, Home Shopping Network, Tivoli Systems, QVC, LA Gear, and Networth. On the other hand there are myriads of losers, and several reasons for their price rise or fall.

Clearly, savvy venture capitalists can benefit from the use of financial astrology. First, there is a large *x* or unknown factor. Estimates vary from only 1 in 10 to 2 in 10 ventures being successful over the long term. How then should a prudent investor choose? Standard market analysis is not possible, and there is always great uncertainty present. Enter the financial astrologer. He/she can improve the odds considerably; we estimate by a factor of two to three times! Even normally skeptical big-money interests are willing to give astrology a try for this purpose, at least once. Someday, astrological analysis of Initial Public Offerings may have become a part of professional due diligence. In fact we are slowly developing the concept of "astrologically certifying" IPOs with a rating of 1 to 5, similar to a value line. In the meantime we recommend the asking of two vital questions.

First, *is the astrological signature valid?* If the entity's line of business isn't prominent, it is far less likely to succeed. Simply study the horoscopes of a number of failed business entities as past verification of this hypothesis. Yes, they may have lacked needed capital, leadership expertise, or strategic vision, or fallen victim to a changing marketplace. But most certainly they also had inappropriate or very difficult horoscope aspects.

Second, *are the first year's astrological transits favorable?* It has been estimated that as many as 50 to 80 percent of new businesses fail within the first year. Everyone would agree that the first year of a new business is critical. This is why astrologers study the transiting planets, especially for the first one to three years, in an attempt to detect potential difficulties. A company may not have sufficient strength to overcome a difficult aspect during its early formative years, while the same aspect will prove far less devastating in its later years.

Some Historical Examples

Microsoft

Almost every investor wishes to find the next Microsoft. It opened at under $2.00 a share, adjusted for splits. One thousand dollars invested on that day would have been worth over $90,000 in 1995! So let's take a brief look at the charts of Bill Gates and Microsoft (see Figs. 8-1 and 8-2).

For starters, astrologers would note the conjunctions of Jupiter–Pluto the north node and Part of Fortune, indicating the possibility of great wealth. Other positions of note are the close Venus–Saturn conjunction, and the Uranus Focus T-Square, with Moon and Mercury–Mars conjunct. On the first trade date of Microsoft we see Jupiter in aspect to the Ascendant, Neptune and Pluto giving a potential for unlimited success, and the Sun with Mars–Uranus for a technical focus.*

---

*According to the Magi Society study of the world's 400 richest people in America in their book *Astrology Really Works,* Bill Gates has the Jupiter–Pluto enhancement, along with Warren Buffet and John Kluge, the three richest American billionaires on the *Forbes* 400 list: "Although Pluto is not associated directly with money per se, it is the planet of power, and money is power....Bill Gates also has the Jupiter enhancement of the Sun, which makes him a very lucky man...and both Buffett and Kluge have the Neptune enhancement of Venus which give them long term moneymaking capabilities."

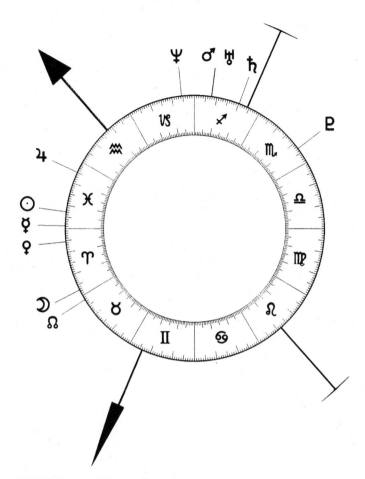

FIGURE 8-1   Microsoft chart.

As a computer user and astrologer, I felt that Windows 95 would have been better as Windows 96. But I was not consulted. However, in the *Forbes* of October 16, 1995, Joan Quigley stated: "Henry Bill Gates III will slip from the top of the *Forbes* list next year, as Microsoft will suffer losses related to ventures into entertainment and may even have to restructure." Quigley believes that "an astrologer consulted for the launch on midnight of August 24, in Auckland New Zealand." Yet if this is the case, most astrologers would agree with me that he/she should be fired for incompetence.

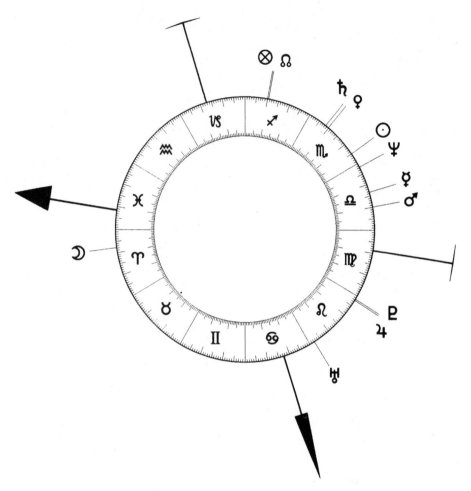

FIGURE 8-2   Bill Gates' horoscope.

Microsoft stock price on August 24   96⅛
Microsoft stock price on October 16   86¾

Netscape

August 9, 1995, is a date investors aren't likely to forget. That is the day Netscape Communications Corp. went public. It offered 5 million shares at $28, then the price shot up to almost $75 during hectic trading before settling at $58.25 by the end of the same day. Its wild gyrations over many ensuing days were equal to the thrills of the futures markets. At the time of writing (Fall '95), Netscape's stock has been wowing the market for months. Yet this 19-month-old company isn't expected to make a real profit for some time.

This is a "story" or "concept" stock in the extreme. On the Internet, like Interactive TV and Multimedia before. Marc Andressen, one of the initial founders, paid $10,860 for the million shares he owns. He can't lose, nor can Jim Clark, who saw his 9.4 million shares top $1 billion dollars in value for the first time on November 17, 1995. The insiders who bought at the opening price and sold the same day for 150 percent profit obviously were happy, but what about the investing public, who bought this IPO on August 9, 1995? Will they *ever* see even $75 in their lifetime? At the time, I would have said never. Yet this was obviously a false conclusion. What does astrology have to say about all this?

We won't refer to the incorporation chart, and show how pre-IPO participants made 150 percent profits in the first hour. We will simply note that those who buy momentum, not value, are happy to "buy at any price." This modern-day South Seas Bubble, or Tulipmania in Holland, attitude perhaps even started the end of one leg of the current bull-market run in technology stocks. Let's look at the calculated at the time of offering 11 A.M., August 9, 1995.

Why, for example, did other winners on the first day of trading, such as Boston Chicken or Home Shopping Network, continue upward? Could it be that these most stellar starts had an auspicious horoscope launch? Yes. Also, while technology stocks are a winning sector, prices simply had gone too far, too fast. Spyglass, which offers its own competitive browser, went public at 17 on June 26, 1995, immediately peaked at 45⅜ until fall of 1995, when it went over 100! Still, a strategy of buying on the first day made money, but not for Netscape public stockholders, at least not initially. Are there astrological reasons for this?

Never Say Never

At the time of the Netscape launch I would have said that the people who invested in Netscape would never see their investment come back to +0. We foresaw serious problems into the second month (see Figs. 8-3 and 8-4). There was a serious security breach, but this did nothing to stop the stock. We forecast astrological/numerology factors present from mid-January to February 1996 that would "cut the price at least in half." Then they announced that they would split the stock at

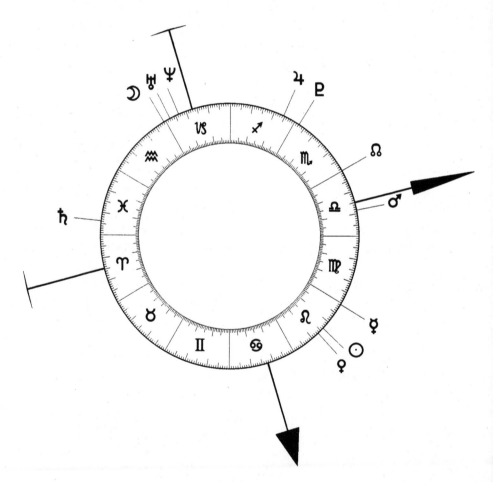

FIGURE 8-3   First trade chart, Netscape.

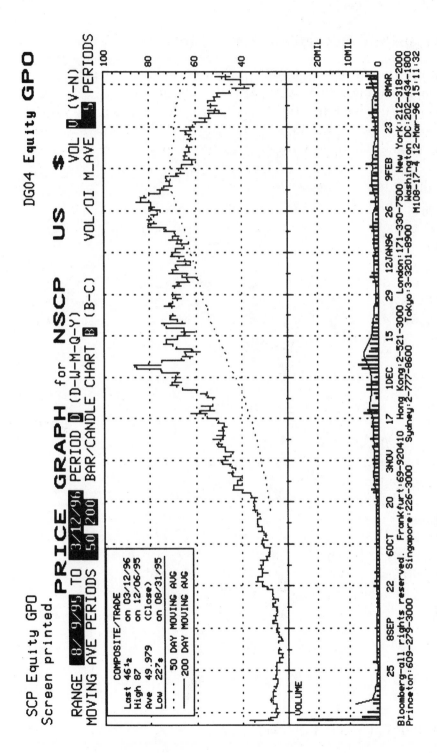

FIGURE 8-4   Technical chart, Netscape. (*Courtest of Bloomberg.*)

the end of January! So we were already half-right, but will we be correct on an adjusted basis? Will these aspects bring sanity to the "Virtual Tulip" pricing mode? Perhaps we'll be wrong again, but that isn't the likeliest scenario. At least we have a "safe time" to short. Sometimes that's all we get from our charting. While this doesn't fully satisfy a long-term investor, it's still *very* valuable to traders.

When the Japanese yen was 105 on its way to 125, we exited between 115 and 120, and I said it would *never* reach 125. Yet markets have a nasty way of getting you. So beware of *nevers* but do *remember* them. Doing so can bring you great opportunities, as with a yen or Netscape short placed at the right time.

We see Mars rising—a key significator for a "hot" stock. Moon (public) Nodes (connects) Uranus (technology) Neptune (anything goes), as well as Mercury–Jupiter–Pluto for potentials of great wealth.

Billionaire for a Day

On November 29, 1995, Steve Jobs became an instant technology billionaire, on paper. Along with Netscape founder James Clark he was briefly a member of the technology billionaire club, proving without doubt that there is money to be made on the Internet. His company, Pixar Animation Studio, made the blockbuster movie *Toy Story*. Investors bought wildly in order to share in the success of the film.

But their joy was short-lived. Had they checked Pixar's first-listing horoscope, they would have noted the prominent Moon–Saturn conjunction. We forecast public (Moon) disappointment (Saturn) in the IPO, and that the stock would fly like a lead balloon. An easy forecast that any financial astrologer could have made (see Figs. 8-5 and 8-6).

Vancouver and Penny Stocks

Similar to emerging markets and IPOs, so-called penny stocks are extremely high-risk ventures. Unlike blue chips, a stock

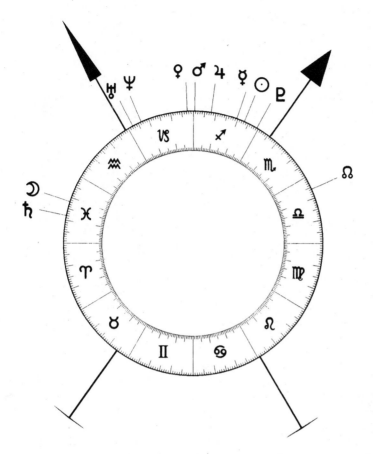

FIGURE 8-5   First trade chart, Pixar.

that falters, rarely if ever recuperates. *Money management* is one's most important activity. Selling 50 percent when a stock doubles, and exiting when 25 to 30 percent down, are two common, virtually ironclad rules for these hot stocks.* High volatility is common. This puts the greatest premium on tim-

---

*If you believe you have a serious long-term winner, however, I recommend the 100/25 percent rule: "At the appropriate time, sell enough shares to cover 100 percent of the initial investment plus 25 percent annualized return." Keep the rest in one's long-term portfolio. Non-experienced or unsophisticated investors, *please be forewarned* of the substantial risks of investing in new startup companies, and be sure to check with your broker or financial adviser beforehand.

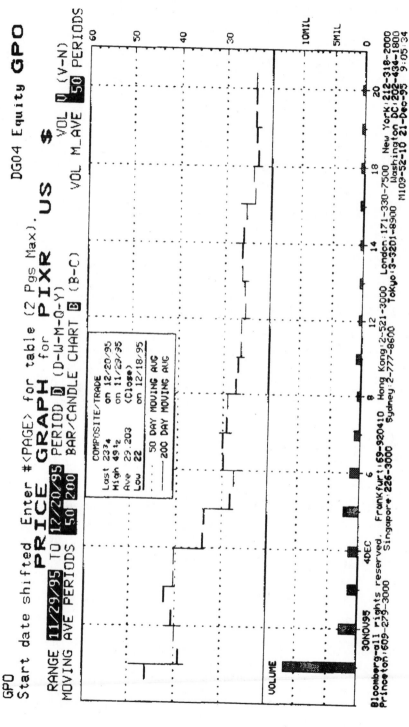

FIGURE 8-6 Technical chart, Pixar. (*Courtesy of Bloomberg.*)

ing. Coupled with extremely low share prices, this is a frequent favorite of beginning astrological speculators.

Follow the Horoscope Road

One client frequently liked to dabble in Vancouver, due to a favorable chart comparison with that exchange/part of the world. Most of the time, I simply ignored these plays and recommendations, except when paid to do astrological work. One phone call on a particular stock was different. I noticed the horoscope-moment that the call was made—something special was in the air. While taking down the horoscope data of the company, I immediately placed an order for 5000 shares, which were executed at less than $.50 CD.

After completing the astrological work and reporting to my client, I took a much larger position, believing that the stock would triple in less than two months and then slowly tailor down. The stock went to $1.90 CD exactly when I had predicted it would. I didn't sell, however. My client was so positive the stock would go to $6+ shortly, that he strongly advised me *not* to sell. He was so enthusiastic that I listened to his advice. The stock fell below $1 CD the next month, just as I had initially forecasted.

I learned two lessons from this experience.

One, even if my astrological forecasts aren't always right, over the long run they provide me with the best way to go.

Two, the reason the stock tripled was that people bought at that price, thinking the stock would move much higher. If that belief hadn't been in the air, the stock never would have reached my target price.

By almost always sticking with my original game plan, I find that over the long run I more often come out a winner.

International Hi-Tech Industries

In November of 1994 we were challenged by a TV reporter to "prove" financial astrology. We eventually answered her challenge as follows: "Suppose I find a company that currently has *no* sales. If I correctly forecast that it will be a billion-dollar company and industry leader within 3 years, would that be good enough for you?" She said that it would.

By serendipity, we were to attend a small analyst's presentation of such a company shortly thereafter. Our investigation procedure is illustrative of our standard methodology.

First we heard a very sexy story, one about a startup company with a revolutionary new product. It was potentially FCB

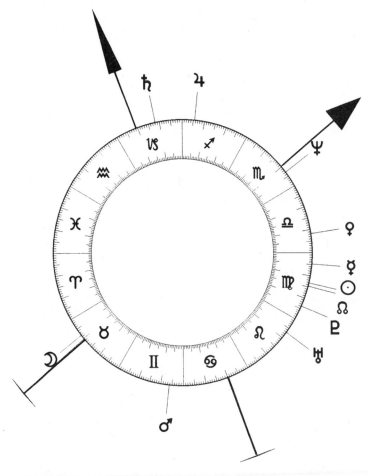

FIGURE 8-7   Horoscope of Roger Rached, president of International Hi-Tech Industries.

(faster, cheaper, and better) than the existing competition. We then looked to the charts of the company, Interna-tional Hi-Tech Industries, and its CEO. Why the CEO? While there is generally agreement between the fortune of a company and its CEO, this isn't always the case. Remember that when the former chairman of Eastman Kodak was forced out, the stock soared. However, this is almost never the case for a startup company. If the CEO is in trouble, there is an almost 100 percent certainty that the company will follow him there. So we took a careful look at the horoscopes of the company and its president (see Figs. 8-7 and 8-8).

Next, industry fundamentals looked highly promising. Here was a high-tech company that could revolutionize the

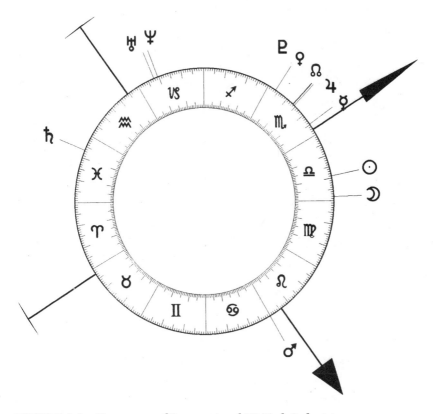

FIGURE 8-8   **Horoscope of International Hi-Tech Industries.**

construction industry just as Microsoft had the computer industry. Obviously there is a huge worldwide demand for buildings and housing. Plus, these buildings were said to be earthquake-, fire-, flood-, and hurricane-resistant! We investigated the company further by having someone knowledgeable in the industry visit its headquarters in Vancouver, B.C., to inspect the high-tech system firsthand. We spoke with the president, not once but many times.

Most important from a purely astrological point of view, the company could potentially take advantage of the upcoming planetary themes: the 1997 Jupiter–Uranus conjunction of high technology, as well as the 2000 Jupiter–Saturn conjunction of Construction.

For all of the above reasons and more, we recommended International Hi-Tech Industries as one of the best new SRI investments for the second half of the 1990s.

Astrologers will easily note the eighth house Virgo stellium in Roger Rached's chart, and the first house Scorpio stellium in the Bermuda chart. Upcoming transits include the Jupiter–Uranus conjunction of February 16, 1997, exactly on the IC of the IHI Bermuda chart.

While no single forecast or prediction can "prove" astrology, if successful this forecast will demonstrate some of the potential power of financial astrology. Critics, please note that if it is *not* successful, it only demonstrates that astrological forecasting is not perfect!

Creating Your Financial Future: A Five-Step Program

Step 1: Realize that Wealth Is More than Money

According to Mark Twain, there are two great tragedies in life. One is *not* getting what you desire in life, and the second *is* getting what you desire!

Many people believe that if only they had just about one-third more money, they would be "happy." Yet if and when they magically obtain that extra money, their desires simply increase, so that they still "require" about one-third more in order to be happy. Not surprisingly, the treadmill of money is just that, a treadmill.

Much of life's precious energy is spent in the pursuit of wealth. Yet countless personal histories attest to how the single-minded pursuit of money resulted in empty, unfulfilled, and unhappy lives. I am not proposing that the lack of money brings happiness, any more than its presence guarantees it. As a rule of thumb I would always go with the majority opinion and prefer the problems that go with money to those that accompany the lack of it. But the pursuit of money *in itself* is vain. Learning how to connect money with your inner, spiritual self will allow you to overcome anxiety and lead to a happier, healthier, and more prosperous life, one that is connected with higher purposes.

It is of course obvious that you won't become an instant

millionaire just through reading this treatise (unless of course that was promised to you in your horoscope!). However, each reader using astrological tools can become *wealthy*. I define a wealthy person as one who has adequate resources to accomplish his or her life-purpose. The trick is to first discover one's life-purpose. Therefore, spend some time deciding what you *really* need, what is of most importance to you. By all means see an astrologer for a horoscope consultation if you like, but there are also many simple psychological exercises that I have used in my astrological practice, which can help to facilitate this discovery process. Four of these are centered around a search for the answer to a question:

1. If you won the lottery today, what life-changes would you make? (First in the short term, then for the longer term.)

2. If you were told you had only one year to live, how would you decide to spend your time?

3. How do you want to be remembered? (The answer to this question can be found by writing your own obituary.)

4. Let's say you have just found a magic lamp, and a genie has granted you three wishes. What are you going to wish for? (*Hint:* If you are at a loss because you can't make up your mind right away, wish to be "healthy, wealthy, and wise" and let the genie figure out what it all means. In other words, see a professional astrologer!)

Do You Want to Become Wealthy?

I'm willing to wager a large sum that you answered "yes"! Yet financial planners say that many of us spend more time deciding which car to buy, or planning a vacation, than defining our financial goals. The first two great obstacles to be overcome are greed and fear. The following series of gestalt exercises may move you forward toward your goals, if you really desire to reach them.

Ten Fear/Greed Exercises

1. Ask yourself, "Fear of *what?* Greedy for what?"

2. Put a face on them. Whose face is it?

3. Give a voice to them. Whose voice is it?

4. How does your fear/greed keep you safe? What *don't* you have to do to remain fearful and greedy?

5. What else would you have to give up, if you gave up fear and greed?

6. What kind of animal is the fear or greed? What does it eat? What kind of animal are *you,* when facing your Fear and Greed?

7. Can you allow your Fear and Greed to exist in you, yet act as if they didn't? What will be the real-world consequences of that approach?

8. What is the opposite of Fear and Greed? Imagine holding the opposites in your right and left palms. What happens?

9. Bring these opposites together. What happens?

10. Imagine holding Fear and Greed in your left and right palms. Bring them together. What happens? (See Fig. 9.1.)

When you work for God the pay is <u>very</u> little...

But the fringe benefits are <u>out</u> of this world!

FIGURE 9.1   Those who work for God.

Step #2: Develop a Winning Strategy

One thing's for sure: there are many *losing* strategies in life and in the markets. As the classic saying goes, "For those who don't know themselves, the market is a very expensive place to learn."

The two worst sins are living in the past and living in the future. Amateurs like to talk about all the money they *could* have made *if*....In our Western, goal-oriented society, the mind usually is focused on the goal rather than on the journey. Tomorrow may come or it may not, but there is rarely any satisfaction to be gained in life, *unless one lives in the present.*

From a purely financial viewpoint, this means planning on the basis of the resources one has *in hand.*

Using astrology for gambling purposes can indeed increase one's chances of winning up to tenfold. Yet I still agree with the comedian who quipped, "The odds of winning the lottery are virtually identical, whether or not one buys a ticket."

As a strong Saturn type, I endorse the Saturnine virtue of simplifying one's life and sticking to the essentials. Another person, true to his or her own horoscope, would define his/her comfort level differently. "Living in the present." "Being true to oneself." Easy to say, not so easy to do. That's why consulting an astrologer is often an important first step toward reaching both your personal and financial goals.

Astrology and SRI Investing

In case the foregoing sections have been too metaphysical for your taste, here's a simpler way to connect your conscience and your pocketbook: SRI Investing.

While the modern era of SRI (Socially Responsible Investing) began with the Vietnam War and the boycott of the racist South African system of apartheid, its origins go back to the Quakers at around the turn of the century. Their major concern was to align their investments with their ethics. Some Quaker churches chose not to invest in companies that made alcohol or tobacco products. This action spawned today's social investment movement, committed to social change and eager to integrate money with ideals. SRI guide-lines or "screens" cover a broad range of factors. SRI analysts study the corporate impacts on their communities, employees, customers, shareholders, and the environment. The goal is one of sound management *and* bringing values to the market-place.

Does SRI investing plus astrology work? Can high princi-ples be brought down to earth? Yes, I believe that adding an SRI screen of social performance to astrological investing can be an easy way to help you hold onto both your pocketbook and your conscience.

Remember, when you're buying stock you're buying not an abstract entity but a company. As a stockholder you are ener-getically connecting with the company and therefore must take some responsibility for its actions. Does that make you comfortable or uncomfortable? If the former, then SRI invest-ing should maximize your comfort level.

Step 3: Choose an Astrological Consultant

I wish to make three basic points about Step #3. First, I believe it is best to choose an astrologer in the same way you would select virtually any professional. Ideally, through a per-sonal recommendation of friends or colleagues. Otherwise, contact a local astrological society or metaphysical bookstore for their recommendation. While membership in a profession-al astrological society doesn't ensure personal quality, at least the person cares enough to be associated with professionals in the field.

Second, when calling for an appointment, ask for a basic profile of the astrologer. Many will send you an information sheet about themselves. Some good questions to ask follow:

Is he or she a specialist in financial astrology? Note that for personal work on your general financial health, timing cycles, potential partnerships, this isn't necessary. But if you have specific questions regarding the financial markets, this may be extremely important, perhaps essential.

Does he or she have other financial qualifications? Just as many counseling astrologers also hold degrees, such as an MA in counseling or an MSW, so an increasing number of financial astrologers also are registered as RIAs, CTAs, etc.

How many years has this person been in practice? With whom has he/she studied? What are his/her professional affiliations? Ask what his/her basic orientation to astrology is, or if he/she has any area of specialization. Get a sense of the basic values of the astrologer, and make sure to ask what you can expect from a session.

Most important of all: If you have some specific goals, fiscal or otherwise, ask in advance how the financial astrologer will help you to reach them.

And yet again: *Let the buyer beware.* In most countries of the world today, astrology is largely an unregulated field. If you are realistic in your expectations, and approach astrology with an attitude both open and critical, I believe you will find it to be equal if not superior to other forms of financial counseling.

Third, while high fees don't necessarily guarantee quality, minimal fees or free readings usually are a tip-off that someone does *not* have professional skills. Someone who undercharges, unless brand-new on the scene and trying to establish a reputation, is automatically suspect, *especially* in financial astrology. Prices vary from community to community, but you can expect to pay from $150 to $300 for a solid, basic astrological consultation in an urban area, and from $100 to $250 an hour, or $250 to $1000 fixed fee, for a financial specialist. Those working as corporate consultants usually charge between $5000 and $25,000 annually, or $1000 to $2000 a month for detailed market advisories.

If you don't feel you require personal attention, the most popular newsletter advisories incorporating financial astrology range from $45 to $500 in their annual subscription fees.

Step 4: Make Your Financial Life-plan Together

One of my favorite pieces of advice is to wear one's portfolio as one does clothing: It should be comfortable, and suited to your personal tastes. Almost any good financial consultant will agree with this principle. Keeping that principle in mind, submit three items to your financial astrologer.

1. Your horoscope data; your birthday, birthplace, and birth time (as known)
2. A list of your financial assets
3. Your fiscal and other life goals

Where astrology can be of especial use is in noting any unusual cycles in your life. Are new financial cycles about to begin? To what extent should you invest in yourself? The horoscopes of successful business owners, executives, and entrepreneurs have distinct astrological signatures. Does the current period suggest rags-to-riches, or financial loss? And so on.

Step 5: Implement Continuous Revision

When one is traveling to a distant location, many plans may have to be changed en route. For example, if we wished to travel to the planet Jupiter in a spaceship, we would have to project where Jupiter would be in relationship to the earth, taking into account the speed of our spaceship, i.e., the time it takes to travel. We would need to constantly reposition the course of our trajectory as we went.

Just so, one's life can benefit from frequent repositioning. Most astrologers, like most doctors and dentists, believe that their clients should come in for regular checkups, but at the very least each new year and on their birthday. If we have "brushed regularly" and had "good dental habits," the visit may be quick and painless. If on the other hand we are out of cosmic harmony, more work will need to be done. Astrology reflects universal connections, and our conscious participation in them can lead us to more joyful and prosperous lives.

The deeper purpose of astrology is something much more than planning and forecasting. It is *creating the future*. It has been said that "the ordinary astrologer predicts the future, the good astrologer helps plan for the future, while the great astrologer helps to create the future." *Exactly.*

Unfortunately, most of today's mundane and financial astrologers don't wield enough powerful influence on a global scale. But as we approach and pass through 1997, with its Jupiter–Uranus and Jupiter–Neptune conjunctions, it is my hope that astrologers will increasingly become empowered to assist humanity in its next step of world evolution. Above all, I hope that *Investing by the Stars* will help *you* to do the same.

Q & A

Broadly speaking there are four types of questions I am regularly asked, variations on "Tell me *how* it is done," "What should I buy/sell in order to make money," "It can't possibly work, can it?", and miscellaneous others. I have answered only those seven that are of the broadest general interest here. Please browse through those that interest you and feel free to submit others to me for inclusion in future editions by writing either to me directly or to one of the Astrologers Funds Internet sites.

1. Does the investor's own natal chart have any relevance?

2. Is the natal chart of the investor/speculator important in determining the timing of investments?

3. Which natal chart(s) are important: The founding of the nation, the exchange, the company whose stock is being considered, or the introduction of the instrument?

4. Can the incorporation chart be timed by the stamp on the articles of incorporation over which the incorporator had no control or even knowledge of?

5. Please explain the most commonly used cyclic pattern, and demonstrate its validity.

6. Can you predict the day-to-day direction of stocks?

7. Can you predict the day-to-day directions of the major market indices and the major commodities for the next few months?

Q: How and why did you become a financial astrologer?

A: While this is quite a long story, I'll keep it relatively short. As I am not a karmic astrologer per se, my story will begin at age six, and not at its probable origins in Atlantis or Phoenicia. Up to that age I manifested a very strong interest in astronomy, but then soon after learning star identification, further studies such as stellar physics left me quite cold.

I then exhibited an unusual talent in mathematics. I was almost always at the top of my math class, with an 800 SAT and the like. I often used to mention my mathematics training in the early days of my career, to help counterbalance the then popular misconception that astrology was a popular superstition, only for the academically untrained and credulous masses. Imagine that! All during my teenage years my love of "pure" mathematics was mixed with an interest in psychology. People, not just abstract ideas, such as Hilbert Space, also seemed important to me.

Now we come to a pivotal moment. I had been introduced to astrology by a girlfriend. I took to it like a duck to water. First, I am a textbook Leo. Almost everything ever written in any sun sign book about the sign Leo (excepting of course, most of the negative character traits!) fits me like a glove. Second, after devouring the classic works of Western civilization (my sister started me on Tolstoy's *War and Peace* at the age of 10), I came to feel more of a natural affinity with Eastern philosophy and Zen, Yoga, Meditation, Gurdjieff, Astrology—all good fodder for NYC Greenwich Village coffee house discussions. Astrology was naturally a part of Indian and Chinese civilization, the two cultures I felt most affinity for. But I still had a Western mindset. The astrological worldview appeared to be nonrational. After all, why should a given moment, whether for a person or a corporation, have *anything* to say about its destiny? Even today I am still constantly amazed, after every reading and successful forecast, that it works so well.

I was sitting in the old Samuel Weiser's bookstore on 13th Street and Broadway in New York City. There was a couch opposite a single bookcase devoted to astrology. I went to pick up a book (fourth shelf from the top). Then, less than 14 inches away, I had a Uranian lightning flash realization: I was *not* really interested in astronomy, mathematics, or psychology, per se, but *astrology*, its common ground. Astrology is properly defined as *a mathematical psychology based on astronomy*. There and then, at that early age, I *knew* what my life's vocation ("calling") was to be. I have never questioned my life-path choice since. Occasionally my route, but never the goal. In typical Plutonic fashion, I devoured every astrology book in sight, and then some. I would choose to skip a meal if it meant being able to buy another book at that moment.

To quickly condense the next 25 years, I set up the NY Astrology Center on the spring equinox of 1968, as a center where people could find qualified astrologers. Then, as now, this is a great problem especially in the United States, with many earnest but undertrained practitioners. I set up ASI Publishers and the NY School of Astrology. We introduced many of the world's top astrologers to the United States, a veritable who's who. I feel especially lucky and blessed to have caught many of the greats in their last years on the planet, and feel sorrow for today's astrologers who never had access to such a stellar group. I wrote textbooks, lectured around the world, etc.

I also became very involved with computers, because astrology is a very labor-intensive field. When I started the average astrologer spent almost half of his or her time calculating horoscopes, not interpreting them. Today, the ratio is better than 15 to 1, and is one of the major reasons for the rise of a professional class from the late 1960s on. Also the fact that thousands of charts can now be calculated and studied, is slowly changing the way astrologers practice. Slowly misconceptions and medieval superstitions are vanishing, but not fast enough for *this* mathematically trained astrologer.

Fast-forward to the October 1987 NYSE crash. I had known about it more than a year in advance (to the day), thanks to Charles Harvey. He along with a host of other financial astrologers, Arch Crawford, and a few Wall Street investment bankers and traders who choose not to reveal their alter ego at that time, made this forecast, which naturally made a great impression on me. The second part of this story was reading about Andy Krieger. He was a currency trader who received much publicity at that time because he had made hundreds of millions of dollars for Bankers Trust, but was unhappy with his meager reimbursement for his efforts. In the middle of the article I had the second lightning-flash intuition of my life: *I could do the same or better!* After all, I made predictions as an astrologer every day of my life. This translated into a directive: *Become a financial astrologer.* Why? Because astrology will gain its mainstream acceptance through the markets. Eventually people will realize not only that financial astrology, but also astrology in general works, and thereby help to spiritually revolutionize society.

I then spent thousands of hours in front of my computer screen calculating and researching the subject of financial astrology. I purposely did *not* read anyone else's work. My training in astrology was superior, but my knowledge of markets was zero. This has allowed me to make some incredible discoveries but also, in my early years especially, some equally incredible blunders. Eventually I made the acquaintance of a number of market professionals to whom I am indebted to for filling in many of the gaps in my knowledge.

My first task was to chart the positive and negative periods of each trading day. My broker told me they were random, and I was certain he was wrong. Within six months he was asking me: "Is this a positive or negative market time?"

I first traded with my own money. As I owned a small computer company, I knew the computer industry inside out. Playing call options on technology stocks in January of 1988 was like shooting fish in a barrel. Often I wouldn't accept 100 percent profits in less than one week—I wanted 200 or 300 percent. How foolish, in retrospect. I played 5, 5, 5 and then 10, 10 and then 20, 20 contracts. Finally I pyramided my winnings to 150 contracts. I figured that if I made more than $100,000 in the first 60 days I "proved" astrology. I allowed them to expire worthless!

Need I say more? I then spent several years constantly

improving my approach, something that worked perfectly, for one market cycle needed adjustment by another. Gradually I also developed quite a unique and precise pricing system—often catching the last tick in SP futures. So much so that when I first began to play futures, I was often the turn point. Later I learned to give more leeway. Of course I continue to learn, but today I believe I have a sufficiently robust system that gives me a considerable edge in calling and trading the financial markets.

Q: Do you use astrology only for forecasting markets?
A: If one does not use astrology, one is missing at least one-third of the market. If I as a financial astrologer don't use fundamental or technical analysis, I may miss two-thirds of the market! Financial astrologers generally are quite confident about the dates on which big market movements will occur, but less confident about which direction—up or down—the particular movement will go in unless they take into account other factors.

As an example, if there is a modest positive Jupiter influence, at a technical support level the market almost certainly will rise. However, it must be a strong one in order to break a technical resistance level, and may result in a flat market.

Q: I went to a psychic, and the stock she recommended lost a lot of money.
A: There are really two parts to this question. The question of horror-scope stories or bad recommendations made by psychics and astrologers is unfortunately all too common. Please remember that financial astrology is a dual specialty, and unless your adviser is knowledgeable about the markets, treat his or her tips and advice the same as you would any other stranger's—with a *lot* of caution.

Second, astrologers are *not* psychics. Astrology is a mathematical psychology based on astronomy. Astrologers use the positions of the planets and the horoscopes (time, place, and

date) of companies and stock markets as the basis of their predictions. Psychics use their psychic ability. Their forecasts can
be wonderfully accurate or woefully absurd, depending on a
number of factors such as whether or not they are having a
good day. A warning: While many psychics are reputable, some
gypsies and con artists masquerade as psychics when their
true interest lies in making money not for you but for themselves. Always exercise caution and take heed of the police
warning: "If it sounds too good to be true, that's probably
because it *is* too good to be true."

Q: Why don't all astrologers agree in their market forecasts?
A: You are presuming that all astrologers should think and act
alike. Not all market technicians are identical in their methodology and techniques, and so with astrologers. Like psycholo-
gists, the practice of astrology varies greatly depending on
where, when, and with whom one has studied. You wouldn't
expect the same counseling styles from a Freudian, Jungian,
or Gestalt therapist, would you?

Of course there are many common elements. We all study
the stars, but may chart them differently. There are also many
different systems of astrology: Chinese, Indian, German, New
York, to name a few, and among these there are many variations as well. Furthermore, it is to a very large extent still
based on an oral tradition. Like acupuncture until recently in
China, there are many "family secrets." Furthermore, in financial astrology in particular, one is not apt to give away one's
best secrets. Finally, because astrology has not been as well
studied in the last two hundred years as other sciences, there
is much discovery work still to be done. Yet it can be a very
powerful tool, even with today's relatively primitive method-
ologies.

Q: Do various markets respond to the same aspect differently?
A: Sometimes. For example, the FT 100 may find a
Mars–Jupiter Square positive fashion, while the SP 500 may
not. This is due to the astrological doctrine of signatures and

the theory of resonance. For example, a native with a strong Saturn won't generally suffer as much difficulty with a Saturn transit (or may indeed be more likely to actually benefit) than say a native with a strong Uranus. This is because the individual with a strong Uranus/freedom urge will feel highly restricted by Saturn, which may bestow stability and reward on its natives. Many U.S. presidents, for example, attained their life goal under Saturn's transit—a reward for hard work and persistence.

Q: Isn't astrology unscientific?
A: Academics often delight in ridiculing astrology as being unscientific. Some years ago 186 scientists, including several Nobel prize-winners, signed a petition against astrology. Yet 95 percent of them had never investigated the subject. More honest researchers, however, who have investigated astrology, have often ended up verifying the astrological hypothesis: that man *is* connected to the cosmos.

There are three primary classes of criticism against astrology.

1. Astronomical

Tropical/Sidereal Zodiac.   Astrologers supposedly ignore the precession of the equinoxes and confuse the signs of the zodiac with the constellations. Therefore the constellation of Aries no longer corresponds to the sign Aries.

Heliocentric/Geocentric.   Astrologers put the earth at the center of their solar system instead of the Sun.

Astrologers are well aware of both of these astronomical facts. While most Western astrologers use a tropical frame of reference, this criticism ignores the majority of Eastern astrologers who do use the sidereal zodiac. Furthermore, many astrologers use both or multiple reference points. For example, the author is not only bi-zodiacal, but uses both heliocentric and geocentric horoscopes. The second criticism was first leveled against astrology at the time of the Copernican revolution, but lost validity after Einstein's theory of relativity blessed any frame of reference. Because we happen to live on the earth, a geocentric (earth-centered) frame of reference makes good sense not only theoretically but where it counts most, in practice.

2. There Are Many Systems and Approaches, Not One

Because astrology has been ignored by mainstream science, there is less codification than would otherwise be the case. Increased worldwide communication among astrologers is slowly improving this situation. However there is also a confusion between "hard" sciences such as physics or chemistry and "soft" sciences such as sociology or psychology. In fact astrology, as a mathematical psychology based on astronomy, is a much "harder" science than most non-physical-based psychologies.

In my *Webster's* dictionary, science is defined as: (1) knowledge obtained by study and practice and (2) any department of systematized knowledge. There is *no* question in my mind that astrology is a science.

Astrology deals with the observation of facts, financial astrology with its correlation to the financial markets. In practice it is much like modern medicine, an art as well as a science. In fact financial astrology is leading the way toward a more scientifically verifiable unified astrological practice.

3. There Is No Satisfactory Explanation of How Astrology Works

"The stars are so far away, how could they possibly influence us?" Believe it or not, this was actually a criticism leveled by astronomers at astrology before the advent of the Space Age. There are many mechanisms in nature that we have no satisfactory explanation for, or else the explanation changes frequently. As for an adequate explanation for astrology's influence, there are a few tentative theories. It's too bad most scientists irrationally boycott it, or we would have better explanations. The big question is: Does astrology *work*? Is it helpful in predicting human (and market) behavior? In my own work, I have found that it is.

Q: Isn't astrology fatalistic?
A: Because many astrologers are quite good at forecasting, it may seem either that they possess special powers, or that astrology is fatalistic. Both assertions are untrue. We won't solve the fate/free will dilemma in one paragraph, but the following points may be helpful.

1. Man does not have unlimited potential. If you have the physical capability of being a great jockey, you can't in the same lifetime have the potential to be a champion basketball player or sumo wrestler. The act of being born itself effects certain limitations.

2. Analogous to weather forecasting, a forecast could be made that it will rain tomorrow, but not the prediction that you will get wet. The choice to take a raincoat or umbrella is yours.

3. A common analogy is made between the birth chart of a individual and the blueprint of a building. Both show a *potential* manifestation, not a certain one.

4. Much of organized religion's opposition to astrology is due to a crucial misunderstanding. The Bible opposes fatalistic interpretations, as do I. God made the heavens as a *sign* for man to use: "The heavens proclaim the glory of God, and the firmament showeth his handiwork."

5. Having the Moon in Libra, I can easily see both sides of an issue. I believe that man has free will but that it is less than he thinks he has, and that often he doesn't even use that! Certainly we appear to have many choices, but not unlimited ones. Anyway, illusion or not, we *act* as if we have free will. Even if astrology is fatalistic, no astrologer is good enough to predict everything correctly. So every prediction has a potential to be wrong. Still, one should always try to be prepared, *especially in the markets.*

Q: I have found a number of astrological forecasts to be wrong and...

A: Why are you expecting astrologers to have perfect records? Like stockbrokers, economists, and meteorologists, astrologers are *not* perfect. In the past the press often used to take a curious delight in pointing out any bad forecasts. A supposed balanced or "objective" view was needed. Yet such a supposedly balanced or "objective" view was missing in similar stories on stockbrokers, economists, or meteorologists.

No astrologer claims to be perfect. We are right often, but not always. Why? Simply because we are human, make mistakes, and are constantly learning. We may base our forecasts on bad or incomplete data (See Appendix II). Finally, no single individual can know *all* there is to know about astrology, and the science of astrology itself is also evolving. Hence we may be surprised by markets, although I would estimate less than half as often as non-financial-astrological analysts are.

In conclusion, I am reminded of the quip: "Why did God create meteorologists? To make economists feel better!"

Q: How about a good horror-scope story?

A: Forgetting about Daylight Savings Time and watching your great, "precise" futures play lose money, because it's off one hour!

Q: Is there a database of significant astrological events?

A: Different astrologers have different opinions about what is significant. A good start is Neil Michelsen's Tables of Planetary Phenomena. See Appendix IV.

Q: Does a financial astrologer look just at current transits, or work with transits and progressions?

A: This depends on their training. Personally I employ quite a large variety of techniques. My choice depends on (1) the nature of the query and (2) how important the query is, i.e., how much work I am willing to do and am I being well paid to do it.

Q: When exactly does a market event take place?

A: This refers to the issues of *orbs*. Every astrological element comes into play by aspect at an exact moment in time. However the orb or influence, that is, its *effect*, is felt both before and after. Depending on the astrological predictive system and the number of timing elements used, this can vary from less than four minutes of time to as much as a year or more.

Q: Tell me a little about how you allocate assets.

A: Our global asset allocation model is based primarily on both country and bourse market horoscopes. These astrological factors help to determine desired relative weighting of funds among the Big Three trading blocks of New York, London, and Tokyo. With increased globalization, we also are increasingly recommending opportunities in other parts of the world, both in secondary and emerging markets. However, given the extreme native volatility of emerging markets, and the severe penalty for being wrong, i.e., wanting to exit in the company of others, the greatest possible care should be taken in the selection process.

Bad Data, Chart Data, Eclipses, and Retrogrades

O ne important issue in any forecasting discipline is the question of data veracity. Another is the fact that one is *always* working with incomplete data. We have mentioned earlier the concept of family horoscopes. I know of no financial astrologer at this time with access to enough supercomputing resources to take in the full range of astrological data of every country, world leader, stock market, stock, etc. Also there is the interesting issue of how the act of predicting the future itself changes the forecast. Certainly in the markets, as astrologers get access to the media, some of their prophecies will become self-fulfilling. Others will be lost to profit. This is one reason why many large fund managers keep their opinions close to their vest, at least until they have accumulated their positions.

Astrological methodology calls for the checking of data through two procedures known as *chart verification* and *chart rectification*. The latter is used when a time of birth is completely unknown, the former when a tentative time is given. The principle is the same: Assuming that astrology works, then the events of life are ordered in a particular sequence. If one were born at a different time, even within a few minutes, the timing sequence would be different or there would be a different set of events. Therefore an astrologer studies a few major events of a life and works backward to see if the chart is valid. Unfortunately this is not only a difficult, but also a not completely reliable procedure. Only when one either gets the same rectification results through more than one qualified astrologer or is able to predict the future with accuracy from the verified time, should one assume that the time is adequate. In

financial astrology, as opposed to the living people, chart verification is a somewhat simpler practice, given the limited
number of possible choices for the life history of a stock.

Probably my most famous wrong forecast was the 1992
Presidential election. I forecasted early on that Bush would
win easily. At least I salvaged some dignity by having also predicted, at the same time, the weeks when Ross Perot would
leave the Presidential race and then reenter it.

When I first made the Bush forecast, two horoscope times
were published for Bill Clinton. One was clearly wrong judging from its astrological signatures; the other seemed okay as
far as his known personality characteristics. I didn't spend the
time verifying his chart by checking the events of his life, as
this was not an important enough forecast for me to warrant
the time required. By the early fall I had begun to suspect that
something was amiss. Candidate Bill Clinton's campaign and
popularity were far too strong, given what I believed his horoscope should have indicted. Shortly after, a third (and accurate) horoscope time for Bill Clinton became public record. It
had a classic winning combination—transiting Jupiter on the
Ascendant—at the time of the November election, among
other favorable augurs.

However, I still felt that Bush *could* win, although certainly not as easily as I first believed, so I let the forecast ride.
Interestingly enough, we did predict that whichever party won
the 1992 Presidential election would lose *dramatically* in the
1994 Congressional elections. I sometimes muse whether
Republican campaign managers knew this as well, perhaps
accounting for how poorly the campaign was allowed to be
run (in my opinion).

Going back to the theory of family horoscopes, using more
than one horoscope to forecast is possible. Given limited time
and resources, I almost always opt for the most recent. The
reason is twofold. First, it is almost always more accurately
timed. For many older charts such as for the United States,
there is still considerable disagreement as to the exact time of
day the Declaration of Independence was signed. Second, it
re-flects the current condition, as does the German reunifica-

tion chart, although earlier charts still operate and may be used when needed when more confirmation is required.

Fortunately, the data of corporations is public record. Unlike Hollywood starlets and a few futures traders, CEOs generally don't try to hide their birth data.

Chart Data for Figures

Chapter 2.

Figure 2-1, Incorporation chart of IBM, 9:00 a.m., May 1, 1958, Albany, NY.

Figure 2-2, First trade chart of IBM, 10:00 a.m., February 14, 1924, Wall Street, NY.

Chapter 3.

Figure 3-1, Peter Lynch's horoscope, 10:51 a.m. September 7, 1943, Boston, MA.

Figure 3-2, Warren Buffet's horoscope, Birth time unknown, August 30, 1930, Omaha, NE.

Chapter 4.

Figure 4-9, Tokyo Stock Exchange horoscope, 9:00 a.m., May 16, 1949, Tokyo, Japan.

Figure 4-10, Japanese horoscope, 12:00 a.m., May 3, 1947, Tokyo, Japan.

Chapter 5.

Figure 5-5, Horoscope chart of Canada, 12:00 a.m., July 1, 1867, Ottawa, Canada.

Figure 5-6, DEC natal chart, 11:30 a.m., August 23, 1957, Boston, MA.

Chapter 6.

Figure 6-1, DEC first trade chart, 10:00 a.m., December 1, 1970, Wall Street, NY.

Figure 6-2, DEC first trade (1987) chart, 7:24 a.m., December 1, 1986, Wall Street, NY.

Figure 6-3, DEC first trade (1995) chart, 5:46 a.m., December 1, 1994, Wall Street, NY.

Chapter 7.

Figure 7-2, IBM horoscope chart, 1995, 7:47 a.m., May 1, 1995, Armonk, NY.

Chapter 8.

Figure 8-1, Microsoft chart, 9:30 a.m., March 13, 1986, Wall Street, NY.

Figure 8-2, Bill Gates' horoscope, 9:10 p.m., October 28, 1955, Seattle WA.

Figure 8-3, First trade chart, Netscape, 11:00 a.m., August 9, 1995, Wall Street, NY.

Figure 8-5, First trade chart, Pixar, 10:50 a.m., November 29, 1995, Wall Street, NY.

Figure 8-7, Roger Rached's horoscope, 3:55 p.m., September 9, 1960, Beirut, Lebanon.

Figure 8-8, International Hi-Tech Industries horoscope, 9:00 a.m., October 4, 1994, Hamilton, Bermuda

PLEASE NOTE: I have posted a number of other charts and horoscopes referenced in this book on my web site under INVESTING BY THE STARTS Additional Data. You may find it on the web in the International Business Journal at: http://www.ids.net/starbridge/afund.

Eclipses, 1996–2001

	LUNAR ECLIPSE	SOLAR ECLIPSE	LUNAR ECLIPSE	SOLAR ECLIPSE
1996	April 4	April 17	September 27	October 12
1997	March 24	March 9	September 16	September 2
1998	March 13	February 26	August 8	August 22
	September 6			
1999	January 31	February 16	July 28	August 11
2000	January 21	February 5	July 16	July 1
		July 31		December 25
2001	January 9	June 21	July 5	December 14
	December 30			

New and Full Moons, Eclipses 1996–2001

	NEW	FULL	NEW	FULL	NEW	FULL	NEW	FULL	NEW	FULL
1996		1/5	1/20	2/4	2/18	3/5	3/19	4/4	4/17	5/3
	5/17	6/1	6/16	7/1	7/15	7/30	8/14	8/28	9/12	9/27
	10/12	10/26	11/11	11/25	12/10	12/24				
1997	1/9	1/23	2/7	2/22	3/9	3/24	4/7	4/22	5/6	5/22
	6/5	6/20	7/4	7/20	8/3	8/18	9/1	9/16	10/1	10/16
	10/31	11/14	11/30	12/14	12/29					
1998		1/12	1/28	2/11	2/26	3/13	3/28	4/11	4/26	5/11
	5/25	6/10	6/24	7/9	7/23	8/8	8/22	9/9	9/20	10/5
	10/20	11/4	11/19	12/3	12/18					
1999		1/2	1/17	1/31	2/16	3/2	3/17	3/31	4/16	4/30
	5/15	5/30	6/13	6/28	7/13	7/28	8/11	8/26	9/9	9/25
	10/9	10/24	11/8	11/23	12/7	12/22				

(Continued)

	LUNAR ECLIPSE		SOLAR ECLIPSE			LUNAR ECLIPSE		SOLAR ECLIPSE	
2000	1/6	1/21	2/5	2/19	3/6	3/20	4/4	4/18	5/4	5/18
	6/2	6/16	7/1	7/16	7/31	8/15	8/29	9/13	9/27	10/13
	10/27	11/11	11/25	12/11	12/25					
2001		1/9	1/24	2/8	2/23	3/9	3/25	4/8	4/23	5/7
	5/23	6/6	6/21	7/5	7/20	8/4	8/19	9/2	9/17	10/2
	10/16	11/1	11/15	11/30	12/14	12/30				

Mercury Retrograde and Planetary Stations, 1996–2001

	MERCURY RX	MERCURY D
1996	January 9	January 30
	May 3	May 27
	September 4	September 26
	December 23	
1997		January 12
	April 14	May 8
	August 17	September 10
	December 7	December 27
1998	March 27	April 20
	July 31	August 23
	November 21	December 11
1999	March 10	April 2
	July 12	August 6
	November 5	November 25
2000	February 21	March 14
	June 23	July 17
	October 18	November 8
2001	February 4	February 25
	June 4	June 28
	October 1	October 23

Venus and Mars Planetary RX and Stations, 1996–2001

	Venus RX	Venus D	Mars RX	Mars D
1996	May 20	July 2		
1997			February 6	April 27
	December 26			
1998		February 5		
1999			March 18	June 4
	July 30	September 11		
2000				
2001	March 9	April 20	May 11	July 19

Jupiter and Saturn Planet RX and Stations, 1996–2001

	Jupiter RX	Jupiter D	Saturn RX	Saturn D
1996	May 4	Sept. 3	July 18	Dec. 3
1997	June 9	Oct. 8	August 1	Dec. 16
1998	July 18	Nov. 13	August 15	Dec. 29
1999	August 25	Dec. 20	August 30	
2000				Jan. 12
	Sep. 29		Sept. 12	
2001		January 25	January 24	
	Nov. 2	(March 1, 2002)	Sept. 26	(Feb. 8, 2002)
		January 24		

Uranus, Neptune, Pluto Planet RX and Stations, 1996–2001

1996	Pluto RX, March 5	Pluto Direct, August 10
	Neptune RX, April 29	Neptune D, Oct. 6
	Uranus RX, May 8	Uranus D, Oct. 9
1997	Pluto RX, March 8	Pluto D, Aug. 13
	Neptune RX, May 1	Neptune D, Oct. 8
	Uranus RX, May 13	Uranus D, Oct. 14
1998	Pluto RX, March 11	Pluto D, Aug. 16
	Neptune RX, May 4	Neptune D, Oct. 11
	Uranus RX, May 17	Uranus D, Oct. 18
1999	Pluto RX, March 13	Pluto D, Aug. 18
	Neptune RX, May 6	Neptune D, Oct. 13
	Uranus RX, May 21	Uranus D, Oct. 23
2000	Pluto RX, March 15	Pluto D, Aug. 20
	Neptune RX, May 8	Neptune D, Oct. 15
	Uranus RX, May 25	Uranus D, Oct. 26
2001	Pluto RX, March 17	Pluto D, Aug. 23
	Neptune RX, May 10	Neptune D, Oct. 17
	Uranus RX, May 29	Uranus D, Oct. 30

Astrological Financial Profile

NAME ——————————— DATE ———————————
ADDRESS ——————————— PHONE (D) ———————————
CITY/STATE ——————————— PHONE (E) ———————————
COUNTRY/ZIP ——————— FAX———————————————

Please answer as fully as possible the following questions. Feel free to communicate any additional information you consider relevant.

1. If you are an experienced investor, how long have you been investing? ——years. Investments you have made. Check all that apply:
——U.S. Stocks————Mutual Funds ——Taxable Bonds
——Tax-free Bonds ———Foreign Stocks ———Short Sales
——Options —————Futures ———Partnerships
——Commodities——Others(s)————————————

2. Which best describes your overall attitude toward investment risk?
—*Strongly risk-averse.* I want only *very* safe investments.
—*Risk-averse.* I do not feel comfortable with risk.
—*Mild risk tolerance.* I am willing to take an occasional risk for above-average gain.
—*Risk taker.* I am willing to take risks with a favorable risk-reward ratio.
—*Strong risk taker.* I am willing to lose a substantial portion of principal in order to *greatly* increase the value of my investment.

3. What are your primary investment objectives? Check all that apply:
—Capital preservation   —Income —Tax Savings   —Growth
—Liquidity

4. What are your main financial goals?
—To be able to retire comfortably
—To provide for the higher education costs of my child(ren)
—To have adequate funds if I should become disabled
—To provide sufficient income for my survivors in the event of my death

_____

_____

5. Please describe your annual profit goals and risk tolerance for funds to be managed by us.

_____

_____

_____

6. How did you hear of us? ———————————————

7. Any comments or additional information you wish to provide:

_____

_____

_____

_____

_____

8. If we reach or exceed our agreed-upon targets, may we use you as a reference?
——Yes———No If yes,——off the record, or ——publicly?

Please include copies of recent statement(s) of any current stock, bond, mutual funds, and futures accounts you wish us to review.

Will be you an active co-participant in managing? If so, complete the following personal astrological data and personal investing history forms.

If you want us to perform a full financial review, please complete the requested information on *all* the following pages. This will allow us to design an investment strategy to help you achieve your long-term objectives.

PERSONAL ASTROLOGICAL DATA

Birth date: —/ —/ — Time:* ——A.M./P.M. Place: ————

*List source: ( ) Birth Certificate ( ) Other

Mother's birth date: —/ —/ — Father's birth date: —/ —/——

Current vocation: ————————————————————

Please list five to seven major life events such as births, deaths, important personal relationships, marriages, divorces, illness, foreign travel, relocation, changes at work or anything else having a major impact on your life. This information will be help us to better serve your needs and will also be used to validate your birth time. The accuracy of this data is essential, so if you are not sure of a date, please indicate that.

Date   Event and personal significance

——/ ——/——   ————————————————
————————————————————————————

——/ ——/——   ————————————————
————————————————————————————

——/ ——/——   ————————————————
————————————————————————————

——/ ——/ ——   _____

_____

——/ ——/ ——   _____

_____

——/ ——/ ——   _____

_____

——/ ——/ ——   _____

_____

PERSONAL INVESTING HISTORY

Please list your two best and worst market trades or investments. Indicate whether you made the decision independently, jointly with an advisor/broker, or on the advice of another.

Entry/Exit   Nature of Trade/Investment
Enter —/ —/ —   Best _____
Exit   —/ —/ —   Decision: ( ) Self ( ) Joint ( ) Others
                           advised
Enter —/ —/ —   Best _____
Exit   —/ —/ —   Decision: ( ) Self ( ) Joint ( ) Others
                           advised
Enter —/ —/ —   Worst _____
Exit   —/ —/ —   Decision: ( ) Self ( ) Joint ( ) Others
                           advised
Enter —/ —/ —   Worst _____
Exit   —/ —/ —   Decision: ( ) Self ( ) Joint ( ) Others
                           advised

1) Have you used a money manager for other than mutual funds in the past? ( ) Yes ( ) No
If yes, briefly indicate your relevant recent results with managed funds:

_____

_____

2) Any past experience with financial astrology? ( ) Yes ( ) No
If yes, describe briefly:

_____

_____

_____

3) Primary time horizon: —Short-term—Intermediate-term —
Long-term

Please fill out this net worth statement *only* if we are doing a
full financial review and you do not have a current net worth
statement to supply. Remember to include recent statements
of any stock, bond, mutual fund, options, and futures
accounts.

NET WORTH FORM

ASSETS	SELF	SPOUSE	JOINT
Cash	———	———	———
Taxable investment	———	———	———
Tax-free investment	———	———	———
IRA/SEP	———	———	———
Keogh	———	———	———
Primary residence	———	———	———
Secondary residence	———	———	———
Other real estate	———	———	———
Personal property	———	———	———
Annuities	———	———	———
Life insurance	———	———	———
Business interests	———	———	———
Misc.	———	———	———
Total	———	———	———

LIABILITIES			
Mortgage	———	———	———
Loans	———	———	———
Taxes	———	———	———
Other	———	———	———
TOTAL	———	———	———

NET WORTH	SELF	SPOUSE	JOINT
Last year's gross income:	——	——	——
Estimate of this year's income:	——	——	——
Annual expenses	——	——	——
Annual savings	——	——	——

Resources

Astrology Books

Gauquelin, Dr. Francoise. *Psychology of the Planets* (San Diego, CA: ACS, 1982). *Rigorously researched list of character traits objectively correlated with each planet.*

Gauquelin, Dr. Michel. *Cosmic Influences on Human Behavior* (Sante Fe, NM: Aurora Press, 1985). *The key pioneering study correlating planetary activity to the biosphere.*

Hand, Robert. *Horoscope Symbols* (Westchester, NY: Whitford Press, 1981). *One of the classics for understanding the planetary symbols.*

Seymour, Dr. Percy. *Astrology: The Evidence of Science,* 2d ed. (London: Arkana, 1990). *Fairly technical "repentance" of a once prejudiced astronomer.*

Weingarten, Henry. *The Study of Astrology,* 5th ed. (New York: ASI Publishers, 1988). *A clear and concise serious approach to the subject.*

Financial Astrology Books

Bates, Graham, and Bowles, Jane C. *Money and the Markets* (London: Aquarian, 1994). *A serious, good second book.*

McWhirter, Louise. *Astrology and the Stock Market,* 2d ed. (New York: ASI, 1977). *A reprint of the pioneering 1930s classic.*

Magi Society, *Astrology Really Works* (Carson, CA: Hay House, 1995). *It looks like one closet financial astrology group is finally opening the door. An interesting and fresh approach to astrology, with a large section on proving astrology through the markets.*

Meridian, Bill. *Planetary Stock Trading* (New York: Cycles Research Publications, 1994). *1000 first-trade charts.*

Mull, Carol. *Standard & Poor's 500* (Tempe, AZ: American Federation of Astrologers, 1984). *500 incorporation charts.*

Mull, Carol. *750 Over-the-counter Stocks* (Tempe, AZ: American Federation of Astrologers, 1986). *750 incorporation charts.*

Market Books

In my opinion, the ideal way to learn is through apprenticeship to some financial guru. Unfortunately this type of access to a financial mentor is not available to all. Second-best may be to study the methods of Wall Street winners. The four classics are:

Schwager, Jack. *Market Wizards* (New York: Harper & Row, 1989).

———. *New Market Wizards* (New York: Harper & Row, 1991).

Train, John. *Money Masters* (New York: Perennial Library, 1994).

———. *The New Money Masters* (New York: Perennial Library, 1989).

Next, I cannot overstress the virtue of sound money management. Therefore I provide here two titles of two books that say almost the same thing, but it is worthwhile to read both to have the points get hammered home.

Eng, William. *Trading Rules, Strategies for Success* (Chicago: Dearborn, 1990).

Sherno, Michael. *Stock Market Rules* (Chicago: Probus, 1994).

These books help you to understand the benefit of gaining a separate understanding of self-worth and net worth:

Needleham, Jacob. *Money and the Meaning of Life* (New York: Doubleday, 1991).
Harrington, John. *Investing with Your Conscience* (New York: John Wiley, 1992).

Finally, the ultimate financial system, perhaps like all others, goes beyond any system:

Toppel, Edward. *Zen in the Markets* (New York: 1992).

At this point I want to recommend reading a few beginners books on trading and investing. Three current favorites are:

Basso, Thomas F. *Panic-Proof Investing* (New York, John Wiley & Sons, 1994).
Cassidy, Donald L. *It's When You Sell That Counts* (New York: Irwin, 1994).
Slatter, John. *Straight Talk about Stock Investing* (New York: McGraw-Hill, 1995).

To find current planetary positions, use an ephemeris or astrological calendar. For serious research, however, access to a computer program is necessary. Contact:

Rosicrucian Ephemerides, 1900-2000, 2000-2100, Rosicrucian, Oceanside.
Tables of Planetary Phenomena, Neil Michelson, ACS, San Diego, 1990.

A wealth of material to research.

Computer Programs

General:
  Matrix Software: Winstar or Bluestar Series
  Paessler Software: Galileo Series
Financial Astrology:
  AIR Financial Trader Program includes 2000 first-trade
charts
  Matrix Compact Data Library:
    Carol Mull's 2500+ corporate charts
    Nick Campion's Book of World Horoscopes

Conferences

The Annual Astrology & The Stock Market Conference, spon-
  sored by The Astrologers Fund, 350 Lexington Ave., New
  York 10016.
Astrology 1995/6, The Free Yearbook of Worldwide Astrology,
  The Urania Trust, 396 Caledonian Road, London N1 1DN
  England (0171) 700 0639. http://www.astrologer.com/
  ut-guide/index.html
International Congress Programs Listing Arcnode "Astro-
  Kring." email: tees.reitsma@astronet.idn.nl

Magazines

Cycles and Business and Investment Cycles, Foundation of the
  Study of Cycles, 900 West Valley Rd., Wayne, PA 19087.
  (610) 995-2120. foundation@cycles.org
Trader's World Magazine often includes astrological contribu-
  tions. Halliker's Inc., 2505 W. Grayrock Drive, Springfield,
  MO 65810. (417) 882-9697. Internet: publisher@
  tradesworld.com

Newsletters

Crawford Perspectives, ed. Arch Crawford. Often rated #1 by timers/trackers. 1382 Third Avenue, #403, New York, NY 10021-0403. (212) 744-6973.

The Astro-Investor, ed. Carol Mull. Gives corporate charts to be in the news. P.O. Box 11133, Indianapolis, IN 46201-0133. (317) 353-6855. Fax (317) 353-6246.

Market Systems, ed. Greg Meadors, Winner of Traders Catalog Trading Contest. 2761 Mansfield Dr., Burbank, CA 91504. (818) 247-1133. Email: meadors@ix.netcom.com.

Financial Astrology Websites

Treasury Consultants Daily Stock Market Report, Treasury Consultants Ltd., P.O. Box 10 Godalming, Surrey GU8 4YW England. Phone/Fax 44 (0) 1428-684325. Email: treasury @dial.pipex.com. URL: http://dspace.dial.pipex.com/town/square/cd61

World Money and Market Trends, Rebecca Nolan, 26A Peel Street G/F Central, Hong Kong. Fax: 852-2850-5502.

Wall-Street-News.Com/Forecasts. Director: Paul Farrell.

Astrologers Fund Forum. Director: Henry Weingarten, www.ids.net/starbridge/afund; or Astrologers Fund on AOL.com or MSN.com.

Both abstract a number of different financial astrologers.

Finding an Astrologer

Directories

1995/96 *International Directory of Astrologers,* ed. Susie Cox. P.O. 43877, Tucson, AZ 85733-3877. (520) 321-1114, susiecox@rtd.com

Metalog

Worldwide on-line directory of astrologers. http:// www.astrologer.com/metalog

Astrological Organizations

AFA: American Federation of Astrologers, P.O. Box 22040, 6535 South Rural Road, Tempe, AZ 85285-2040. (602) 838-1751. afa@msn.com

AFAN: Association for Astrological Networking, 8036 Wilshire Boulevard, Suite 537, Beverly Hills, CA 90211. (800) 578-AFAN.

Astrological Association, Secretary: 396 Caledonian Rd., London N1 1DN, England. (0171)700 3746. http://v/ www.astrologer.com/aanet

APA: Association of Professional Astrologers, c/o Annette Platts, 22 Ruth Close, Cove, Farnborough, Hants, GU14 9UX, England.

NCGR: National Council for Geocosmic Research, c/o Mary Downing, Box 1220, Dunkirk, MD 20754. (410) 257-2824. ncgr@allware.com. http://www.allware.com/ncgr

PROSIG: Professional Concerns, c/o Monica Dimino, 195 Eadenfield Ave., Watertown, MA 02172. (617) 923-6424.

Wall Street Games

Practice trading and investing with play money. It can be fun, and most often will save you money in the long run.

Stock Games on the Net

IFBG Stock Market Simulations Games, http:// www.wiso.gwdg.de/ifbg/stock4.html
Source of a number of Wall Street games on the Net.

Futures

Auditrack. 309 SE Mizner Blvd., Suite #62, Boca Raton, FL 33432. (407) 393-3876. *Audiotrack is a professional simulated brokerage that provides traders with the opportunity to develop real-time track records with hypothetical funding.*

Other Information Resources

SAFTI: Society of Asset Allocators and Fund Timers, Inc., 11275 East Mississippi Avenue, Suite 2-E3, Aurora, CO 80012. (714) 476-2799.

SIF: Social Investment Forum, P.O. Box 57216, Washington, DC 20037. (202) 872-5319.

Srb Internet Socially Responsible Mailing List Discussion Group, Subscribe SRB Listproc@mail.together.net
Email: SRB@bristlecone.together.net

Foundation for the Study of Cycles, 900 West Valley Road, Suite 502, Wayne, PA 19087-1821. (610) 995-2120. foundation@cycles.org

New York Astrology Center, 350 Lexington Avenue, #402, NYC 10016-0909. (212) 949-7211. Fax: (212) 949-7274. Email: AFund@AOL.com,http://www.IDS.NET/Starbridge /AFUND *Currently the single best worldwide source of books, software, and current information on financial astrology and astrology in general.*

Glossary

Astrological Terms

Ascendant: References the moment an entity is born. One of the four personal points in astrology, along with the Sun, Moon, and Midheaven. All of them are key indicators of individual expression.

Aspect: The angular relationship among planets. When planets are in "aspect" they are in relationship, and affect each other's possible/probable manifestations.

Astrology: A mathematical psychology based on astronomy.

Conjunction: Two or more planets are said to be "conjunct" when they are in the same part of the sky.

Disaster: Dis = away; *astres* = the stars. Disasters are more likely to occur when one is *not* aligned with one's horoscope, i.e., when one tries to fit a round peg into a square hole.

Electional: The branch of astrology that deals with "electing" or choosing a favorable time to commence activities, such as marriage, incorporating a company, or arranging a business meeting.

Feng shui: Literally, wind and water. Refers to one of a number of Chinese practices to align human activity with the earth and cosmos.

Horary: Horos means *hour,* and therefore this is the branch of astrology that answers questions by referring to the time when the question was asked.

Horoscope: From the Greek—horos: hour; skopos: map. A birth chart references a unique time/place event, company, or person.

Midheaven: References the moment an entity is born. While the ascendant aligns to the eastern horizon, the midheaven is the second dimension aligning to the highest point a planet reaches in its daily motion.

Mundane astrology: The branch of astrology that deals with "mundane" or worldly matters. Its primary concerns are political, economic, financial, and geophysical events and trends, correlating to planetary activities.

Natal horoscope: Another name for the birth horoscope.

Orb: Refers to the exactness/inexactness of an astrological aspect or event.

Retrograde: Refers to the *apparent* backward motions of the planets. Purely a geocentric phenomena, as the planets are always direct in their motions.

Rulerships: Correspondences of the planets and signs of astrology to various phenomena.

Stationary: Refers to the apparent stationary or stopped motion of planets. Purely a geocentric phenomena, as the planets are always moving forward in their orbits.

Synastry: Syn: with; astres: the stars. The branch of astrology that deals with relationships between people, companies, countries, etc.

Transits: The primary tool of predictive astrology. Refers to the current state of the planets at the birth moment or natal horoscope.

Financial Terms

Arbitrage: Making a profit by simultaneously buying and selling related contracts that are out of synchronization, buying the cheaper or undervalued instrument and selling the more expensive or overvalued one.

IPO: Initial public offering of stock.

Contrarian investing: A market approach that is contrary to market action: buying when others sell, selling when others buy.

False bottom: A technical support point that is broken by subsequent market action.

False top: A technical resistance point that is broken by subsequent market action.

Growth investing: A market approach that looks to stocks with above-average projected earnings.

Relative strength: Performance relative to a benchmark, such as the S&P 500.

Shorting stock: Selling stock *in advance* of its purchase. In contrast to the usual practice of buying stock in anticipation of its increase in value, a stock is shorted or sold first when anticipating a price decline, with the expectation of purchasing it at a later date at a lower price.

SRI: Socially responsible investment.

Value investing: A market approach that looks for low p/e, or price-earnings, ratios.

XAU: An index of leading gold and silver stocks.

Volatility: One index of price movement of stock and option fluctuations.

Index

Abelson, Alan, 101
Acquisitions and mergers, 122
Adams, Evangeline, 15
Advance information, 3–4
Aerospace industry, planetary
    rulers, 36, 40
Agriculture, planetary rulers, 36–37
    (*See also* Commodities)
Apparel industry, planetary ruler-
    ship, 36
Applied technology, 94
Aquarius, corporations in, 8–9, 56,
    130–131
Arabic astrology, 36–37
Arguilles, Jose, 99
Aries, corporations in, 8, 56,
    129–131
Aspects, planetary, 35, 55, 60, 89,
    192–193
    (*See also individual planets*)
Asset allocation, 53, 197
Astrologer:
    author profile, 187–191
    classical vs. computer-based
        modeler, 72
    guidelines for choosing, 183–185
    historical status, 14–19
    requirements for success, 22–26,
        31, 33
    vs. psychic, 191–192
Astrology:
    accuracy of, 196, 199–204
    definition, 189
    forecasting methods, 44–47

Astrology (*Cont.*):
    and free will, 195
    philosophical view, 9–11
    planetary rulership, 36
    and psychology, 6, 25–26, 35–36,
        136–137, 194
    purposes of, 4–6, 185–186
    as science, 193–195
    (*See also* Financial astrology)
Astronomical Cycles Sum, 98–99
Australia, and currency trading,
    112
Autumn, and market patterns, 73
Aviation, planetary rulers, 36, 40

Banking industry, planetary rulers,
    34, 36
Barings Bank crisis, 88
Baruch, Bernard, 143
Barycenter, 76
Belief, power of, 20–21
    (*See also* Self-fulfilling prophecy)
Birth chart (*see* Natal horoscope)
Bond market, 78, 116–117
Buffet, Warren, 56–59
Business use of astrology (*see*
    Financial astrology)
BusinessWeek, astrological origins,
    15

Calls, trading, management of,
    137–138, 143–144

Canada, investment in, 113–115, 175

Cancer, corporations in, 8–9, 34, 56, 130–131

Capital, importance in trading, 24–25
(*See also* Money management)

Capricorn, corporations in, 8–9, 56, 130–131

Career choices, and astrology, 5–6

CEO (Chief Executive Officer), weighting of horoscope, 177

Change, cyclical nature of, 73

Chemical industry, planetary rulers, 36

Chinese astrology, 20–22, 73, 75, 83

Client profile, 50, 56–60, 205–210

Closed vs. open funds, 128–129

Commodities, 36–37, 76–77, 80

Computer industry, planetary rulers, 36
(*See also* Technology stocks)

Computer trading, in stock analysis, 41, 123

Concentration vs. diversity of investments, 53

Confluence of effects, as indicator of major events, 70–71

Conjunctions, planetary (*see* Aspects, planetary)

Contrarian trading, 139–140, 156

Corporate damage control, astrological role, 157

Corporations, sun signs for, 8–9

Correspondences (*see* Rulerships, planetary)

Cosmetics industry, planetary rulers, 36

Countertrend trading, 139–140, 156

Crawford, Arch, 16, 18, 189

Cross-market confirmation, 39

Currency trading, 85, 109, 112, 155–156

Cycles, astrological and market, 29, 41–43
calendar cycle, 150
and industrial groups, 94–95, 120
in investment strategy, 73–83
lunation, 82
and October 1987 crash, 93–96
planetary influence on, 34–35
vs. technical, 150–151

Daily predictions, astrological approach, 65–66, 87–88, 138–139

Data veracity, and astrological forecasting, 199–204

DEC (Digital Equipment Corp.), 123–126, 146–148

Defense industry, planetary rulers, 36

Derivatives, rise of, 41

Dharma, as guide to fulfillment, 5

Digital Equipment Corp. (DEC), 123–126, 146–148

Diversity vs. concentration of investments, 53

DJIA (Dow Jones Industrial Average), 40–43, 118, 122–123

Doctrine of signatures, 35, 122, 165–166, 192–193

Dollar, Canadian, technical analysis, 113

Dollar-cost-averaging strategy, 127

Dow Jones Industrial Average (DJIA), 40–43, 118, 122–123

Earning surprise, 155

Eclipses:
dates for, 201–202

Eclipses (*Cont.*):
  as indicators of market movement, 66
  and lunation cycles, 82
  and October 1987 crash, 67, 69
  and options trading, 151
  and volatility prediction, 89
Economic cycles (*see* Stock markets, cycles in)
Elections, U. S., astrological insight into, 121, 200
Emotional life, astrology as enhancer of, 11
Entertainment industry, planetary rulers, 36
Environment, as life influence, 11
Ephemeris, definition, 65
Equinox charts, and options trading, 150
Event vs. market prediction, 89
Exact mathematical space forecasting, 44

Fall season, and market patterns, 73
False bottoms, predicting, 84–86
False tops, 85
Family horoscope theory, 39, 112–116, 118, 200–201
Fatalism, and astrology, 195
Fear/greed, analysis of, 181
Feng Shui, 20
Financial astrologer (*see* Astrologer)
Financial astrology:
  cycles in, 29, 41–43, 73–83, 93–96, 120, 150–151
  growth of, 19–22
  history of, 15–19
  and principles of investment, 38–39
  purposes of, 11–15
  (*See also* Technical analysis)

Financial consultant, role of, 47
  (*See also* Astrologer)
Financial planning strategies, 179–186
Financial services, planetary rulers of, 36
Financial Times Stock Exchange (FTSE), 91–93
First listing date, analysis of, 8–9, 29, 145
Five percent rule, 53
40 month cycle, in stock market, 81
The Foundation for the Study of Cycles, 19, 83
Free will, and astrology, 195
FTSE (Financial Times Stock Exchange), 91–93
Fundamental analysis, astrological role in, 25–27, 122, 135, 177–178
Futures trading, 18–19, 41, 148–153

Galactic Center, and market crashes, 69–70
Gaming/casino industry, planetary rulership of, 40
Gann, W. D., 15, 66–69, 75–76, 94
Gates, Bill, 166–168
Gauquelin, Michel, 5
Gemini, corporations in, 8–9, 56, 130–131
Geocentric vs. heliocentric view, 193–194
Geopolitical events, astrological role in, 23–26, 88–89, 121, 159–160, 200
Gold stocks, 112, 128
Gorbachev, Mikhail, 160
Graham, Benjamin, 56–59
Grain markets, 160
Greed/fear, analysis of, 181
Growth investing style, 56–59

Guidepost theory, 44

Harding, Michael, 90, 93
Harmonic Convergence, and
    October 1987 crash, 67–70, 99
Harvey, Charles, 16, 189
Healthcare industry, planetary
    rulers, 36
Hedge-fund managers, financial
    astrologers as, 3
Hedging vs. speculation in options
    trading, 151
Heliocentric vs. geocentric view,
    193–194
Heredity, as life influence, 10–11
Hong Kong, astrological influence
    of, 20
Horary astrology, 61–63
Horoscopes (*see specific types*)
Household products, planetary
    rulers, 36
Hulbert, Marc, 18

IBM (International Business
    Machines Corp.), 30–31,
    40–41, 122–123, 157–159
Incorporation date, importance of,
    8, 12, 29–30
Indicators, rules for handling,
    38–39, 144–145
Industrial machinery, planetary
    rulers for, 36
Industry groups:
    and mutual funds, 126–131
    planetary rulers, 36–37
    and political events, 121
    selection guidelines, 118–120
    weighting of, 107
Inflation, and market selection,
    116–117
Initial Public Offerings (IPOs),
    165–178

Insider information, 3
Interest rates, 76–77, 155–156
International Hi-Tech Industries,
    175–178
Intersection theory, 40
Investment styles, 46–52, 54,
    56–59
IPOs (Initial Public Offerings),
    165–178

Jayne, Charles, 70–71
Jones, Paul Tudor, 59, 144
Jupiter:
    characteristics of, 34–35
    and industry groups, 119–120
    and investment style, 55, 57
    and Neptune aspects, 40, 85
    retrograde and planetary stations
        of, 203
    rulerships of, 36
    and Saturn aspects, 67, 73–78,
        80, 94–96

Karma, in financial astrology, 23
Kondratieff, N. D., 75

Leo, corporations in, 8–9, 34, 56,
    130–131
Libra, corporations in, 8–9, 56,
    130–131
Life-purpose, importance of, 10, 180
Locality factor, 5, 13
London stock market, 91–93
Long cycles in stock market, 75–79
Love, astrology's contribution, 4–5
Lunation cycle, 79, 82, 150–151
Lynch, Peter, 56–58

Market selection (*see* Stock selec-
    tion)

Market timing (*see* Timing of markets)

Markets (*see* Stock markets)

Mars:
  as key influence on stock market, 93, 95
  and Neptune midpoint, 61
  and October 1987 crash, 67, 69
  retrograde and planetary stations of, 203
  and risk tolerance, 51
  signatures of, 35–36
  and value investment style, 57

Master Time Cycle, 94–96

Master Time Factor, 75–79

Meadors, Greg, 18, 82–83

Meaning of life, 10, 180

Media industry, 16–19, 36, 156–157

Mercury, positions and influences, 36, 202

Mergers and acquisitions, 122

Meridian, Bill, 145–146

Merrill Lynch, use of astrology, 21

Mexican economic crisis, 108–111, 115

Microsoft Corp., 166–168

Mineral resources, planetary rulers, 36

Money:
  emotional attitudes to, 22
  vs. wealth, 179–182

Money management:
  and financial astrology, 22–26
  general guidelines, 133–135
  in market trading, 138–141
  in penny stock investment, 173, 175

Moon, positions and influences, 36, 79, 82

Morningstar Five-star Funds, 130–131

Multiple trading systems, 33, 43, 45, 152

Mundane astrology, 121

Mutual funds, 41, 126–131

NAFTA (North American Free Trade Agreement), 108, 111

Natal horoscope:
  birth data availability, 58–59
  in currency trading, 112
  function of, 28–31
  and individual potential, 11, 25, 29–31, 38
  in market timing, 33

Nelson, J. H., 67

Neptune:
  and investment style, 55
  and Jupiter aspects, 19–20, 40, 85
  and Mars at midpoint, 61
  retrograde and planetary stations of, 204
  rulerships of, 36
  and Saturn aspects, 84–85, 101, 104–105
  and Uranus aspects, 16–17

Netscape Communications Corp., 168–172

New Age movement, astrology's growth and, 14

New York Stock Exchange (NYSE), 40–41, 68, 118

Nikkei Index (*See* Tokyo Stock Exchange)

1987 stock market crash, 15–16, 67–70, 74, 90–101

1929 stock market crash, 15

Numerology, 69–70, 77

NYSE (New York Stock Exchange), 40–41, 68, 118

October 1987 market crash, 15–16, 67–70, 74, 90–101

Open vs. closed funds, 128–129

Options trading, 99, 148–151
Options-expiration day, 141–142, 150
Orange County, California, 156
Orbs, definition, 197

Pattern recognition in market forecasting, 28–29, 33
Penny stocks, risks of, 172–173, 175
Persian Gulf War, 23–24, 88–89
Personnel hiring, astrological uses in, 12–13
Peso, Mexican, 109
Pharmaceuticals industry, planetary rulers, 36
Pisces, corporations in, 8–9, 56, 130–131
Pixar animation studio, 172–174
Planetary influences:
    confluence of effects, 7, 70–71
    daily analysis, 65–66
    evidence for, 76–79
    indicators for, 72
    on industry groups, 118–120
    on investment style, 54
    outer vs. inner planets, 70–71, 120
    and transits, 33
    trigger effect, 161
    (See also Aspects, planetary; Cycles, astrological and market)
    (See also specific planets)
Planned trading, 138–139, 175
Pluto, positions and influences, 34, 36, 154, 204
Political events, astrological insight into, 23–26, 88–89, 121, 159–160, 200
Position vs. day trading, 138–139, 175
Potential, importance of natal, 25, 29–31, 38

Precious metals, planetary rulers, 34, 36
Press industry, 16–19, 36, 156–157
Price/earnings ratios (P/E), attitude to, 56–57
Profits, handling of, 141–145
Program trading, and stock analysis, 41, 123
Progressions vs. transits analysis, 196–197
Psychic vs. astrologer, 191–192
Psychology and astrology, 6, 25–26, 35–36, 136–137, 194

Quigley, Joan, 167

Rached, Roger, 176–177
Real estate market, astrological analysis, 36, 104, 119, 126
Recreation, planetary rulers, 36
Rectification of chart, 199–201
Reincarnation, 10
Reinforcement theory, 40
REITs (Real Estate Investment Trusts) (see Real estate market)
Relationships, charting of, 4–5, 49–52, 63–64, 121–122, 153
Religion, opposition to astrology, 195
Resonance, theory of, 193
Restaurants, planetary rulers, 36
Retailing, planetary rulers, 36
Retrograde cycles and positions, 82, 202–204
Risk tolerance, analysis of, 50–51
Risk/reward ratio, 140, 151
Rulerships, planetary:
    business application, 34–38
    changing nature of, 40
    and vocational choice, 5–6
    (See also specific planets)

Sagittarius, corporations in, 8–9, 56, 130–131
Saturn:
  characteristics of, 34–36
  and corporate downsizing, 120
  and Galactic Center, 69–70
  and Jupiter aspects, 67, 73–78, 80, 93–96
  and Neptune aspects, 84–85, 101, 104–105
  retrograde and planetary stations of, 203
  and risk tolerance, 51
  and value investment style, 57
Science, astrology's status as, 193–195
Scorpio, corporations in, 8–9, 56, 130–131
Self-fulfilling prophecy, 21, 199
Self-knowldege, as key to better decision-making, 6
Selling stock, timing of, 52, 146–151
Short cycles, trading influences, 79–83
Shorting of stocks, strategies for, 146–151
Sidereal potential line, 98
Sidereal vs. tropical Zodiac, 193
Signatures, astrological, 35, 122, 165–166, 192–193
60-year cycle, significance of, 94
Socially Responsible Investing (SRI), 182–183
Solar cycle, 150
  (See also Sun, influences; Sun sign astrology)
Solar Return horoscope, 157
Solstice charts, and options trading, 150
Soviet Union, Gorbachev coup attempt, 160
S&P Money Center Banks, 32

Speculation vs. hedging in options trading, 151
Spiritual life, astrology as enhancer of, 11
Splits of stock, 145
Sports, planetary rulers, 36
SRI (Socially Responsible Investing), 182–183
Steel, planetary rulers, 36
Stock exchanges, sun signs for, 7–8
  (See also individual exchanges)
Stock markets:
  cycles in, 28–29, 41–43, 75–83, 150–151
  dynamic elements, 27, 43
  forecasting with astrology, 89, 191–192
  handling hot issues, 145–146
  high/low chart analysis, 83–85
  and interest rate influence, 76–77, 155–156
  planetary relationship to, 34
  variation in international, 93
  weighting of, 107–112
  (See also Timing of markets)
Stock selection:
  and industry groups, 117–121
  inflation considerations, 116–117
  mutual funds, 126–131
  strategies for, 47, 107–116
  by sun sign, 8–9, 56
  technology stocks, 122–126
Stops, strategy for using, 140–141
Sun, influences, 36, 76, 89
Sun sign astrology, 5–9, 55–56
Surprises, market, 155
Synastry, 49–52, 63–64, 121–122, 153
Systems planning approach, 14–15

Taurus, corporations in, 8–9, 56, 129–131

Taxes, influence on markets, 41
Technical analysis:
  astrological role in, 25–26, 33,
    151–153
  astrology's similarity to, 117
  in confirmation of trade, 39
  and first listing date, 145
  importance of, 135
  and market dynamics, 27
Technology stocks:
  author's experience with, 190
  DEC analysis, 123–126
  IBM, 30–31, 40–41, 122–123,
    157–159
  International Hi-Tech Industries,
    175–178
  Microsoft Corp., 166–168
  Netscape Corp., 168–172
  Pixar animation studio, 172
  planetary rulers, 36, 122n
Telecommunications industry, 36,
  111
Telemex, 111
Theme investing, 38
Timer vs. trader, 141
Timing of markets:
  astrological role in, 11–12,
    25–26, 47, 60, 135–137
  importance of, 38
  influential elements of, 41
  and knowing yourself, 49–52
  in options trading, 149–150
  stock-picking strategy, 107–108
  transits as tool for, 33–34
Tokyo Stock Exchange, crash of,
  83–86, 101–105
Top-down approach to stock-picking, 107–108
Toronto Stock Exchange, 114
Trader vs. timer, 141
Trading strategies:
  call management, 61–63,
    137–138, 143–144
  computer trading, 41, 123

Trading strategies (*Cont.*):
  contrarian, 139–140, 156
  currency trading, 85, 112,
    155–156
  daily vs. position, 138–139
  importance of capital, 24–25
  multiple systems, 33, 43, 45,
    152
  options trading, 99, 148–151
  and synastry, 63–64, 153
  (*See also* Futures trading; Money
    management)
Trading vs. trending market modes,
  153–154
Transits, 29–33, 166, 196–197
Transportation, planetary rulers,
  36
Trending vs. trading market modes,
  153–154
Trigger effect, in planetary influence, 70–71, 96, 161
Triple-trading-screen model, 33, 43,
  45, 152
Tropical vs. sidereal Zodiac, 193
20-year cycle, significance of,
  94–95

Underdeveloped countries, risks of
  investment, 116
Universe, interconnectivity of,
  9–10
Uranus:
  and harmonics with Venus, 69
  as key influence on stock market,
    93–96
  and Neptune aspects, 16–17
  retrograde and planetary stations
    of, 204
  rulerships, 35–36, 162
  and volatility prediction, 89

Value investing style, 56–59

Vancouver, BC, investment in, 175
Venture capitalism, 55, 165–178
Venus, positions and influences, 36, 51, 67, 69, 203
Verification, chart, 199–201
Virgo, corporations in, 8–9, 56, 130–131
Vohrzek, Mary, 60–61

Volatility in markets, 89–90, 150–151, 173, 175

Wealth creation vs. preservation styles, 50–51
Wealth vs. money, 179–182
Williams, David, 97

About the Author

Henry Weingarten, a professional astrologer for 28 years, founded the New York School of Astrology. He is managing director of the Astrologers Fund, in which role he advises leading Wall Street money managers, traders, and private investors. His timely forecasts have included: The Tokyo Market Crash, US Mideast War, the failure of the Russian Coup, and the Mexican market crashes. He has been a professional computer systems designer and is currently developing an artificial intelligence model for astrology. His work has since been featured in such publications as *Business Week, The New York Times, The Wall Street Journal, Financial World,* and *Barron's.* Weingarten, a Leo, lives in New York City.